THE WHITE MAN'S BURDEN

THE WHITE MAN'S BURDEN

A Play In Two Acts

By

PAUL THEROUX

HAMISH HAMILTON · LONDON

All rights in this play are strictly reserved, and application for performance etc. should be made, before rehearsals, to Harvey Unna & Stephen Durbridge Ltd, 24 Pottery Lane, Holland Park, London, W11 4LZ

HAMISH HAMILTON LTD

Penguin Books Ltd, 27 Wrights Lane, London W8 5TZ (Publishing & Editorial)
and Harmondsworth, Middlesex, England (Distribution & Warehouse)
Viking Penguin Inc., 40 West 23rd Street, New York, New York 10010, U.S.A.
Penguin Books Australia Ltd, Ringwood, Victoria, Australia
Penguin Books Canada Limited, 2801 John Street, Markham, Ontario, Canada L3R 1B4
Penguin Books (N.Z.) Ltd, 182–190 Wairau Road, Auckland 10, New Zealand

First published in Great Britain 1987 by
Hamish Hamilton Ltd

British Library Cataloguing in Publication Data
Theroux, Paul
The White man's burden.
I. Title
812'.54   PS3570.H4

ISBN 0-241-12240-6

Typeset by Eta Services (Typesetters) Ltd, Beccles, Suffolk
Printed and bound in Great Britain
by Butler & Tanner Ltd, Frome & London

CAST

Rudyard Kipling, 31

Caroline ("Carrie") Kipling, 34

Matthew Howard, 45, Kipling's coachman

Mary Hackett, 25, a journalist

Beatty Balestier, 27, Carrie's brother

Dr. James Conland, 50, the Kiplings' physician and close
friend

Mrs Anna Balestier, 62, Carrie's mother

William Newton, 80, a judge

Clark C. Fitts, 35, a lawyer

George Hitt, 30, a lawyer

(Balestier is pronounced in the American way, "Balla-steer".)

The play takes place in Kipling's house "Naulakha", in
Brattleboro, Vermont, in 1895 and 1896.

Act One
Scene 1. Naulakha, mid-December, 1895.
Scene 2. The same, Christmas Day.

Act Two
Scene 1. Naulakha, Spring, 1896.
Scene 2. The same, a week later.
Scene 3. Brattleboro Town Hall, May 12.

AUTHOR'S NOTE

I had finished my South American travel book, *The Old Patagonian Express*, and was wondering whether I had the courage to begin a novel (it was *The Mosquito Coast* and I suspected it would take two years), when a fairly well-known theatrical director asked me whether I had ever considered writing a play. This was just what I needed to help me procrastinate. I told him truthfully that I had begun as a writer with one-act plays and as a twenty-year-old had often sat with a skein of pipesmoke around my face thinking of myself as "poet-playwright".

And I had an idea: the Kipling business in Vermont that is glossed over in his biography. I was attracted to it because I am fascinated when people are revealed to be acting totally out of character. This was a vivid instance of it. Kipling, whose law was one of peace-making and magnanimity, had become embroiled in a family row over money and his brother-in-law had threatened to kill him. At the time, Kipling and Robert Louis Stevenson were the most famous writers in the world. This was 1894 – and they were both young, both far away from home (Vermont and Samoa) and both married to Americans.

The director liked the idea and commissioned me to write the play. That was the end of 1978. The next three or four months were among the happiest I have known as a writer. My travel book was done. My novel *Picture Palace* had just appeared; and I had this great idea. I went to Brattleboro, Vermont, and traipsed around Kipling's house, "Naulakha". I interrogated Angus Wilson, who had just written a biography of Kipling; and I made trips to the newspaper library in distant Colindale, in north London. Then I was done. I delivered the play in person and the director said he was eager to read it.

A month later he still had not read it. More weeks passed. I began to write short stories. None of them was about a theatrical squirt, but one was about the monotonous hell of waiting for a verdict.

Waiting . . . reminded Harper of his childhood, which was a jumpy feeling of interminable helplessness. And childhood was another country, too, one governed like this by secretive people who would not explain their schemes to him. He suspected as a child that there were rules he did not know. In adulthood he learned that there were no particular rules, only arbitrary courtesies. Children were not important, because they had no power and no menace: it took a man twenty-eight years to realize that. You wait; but perhaps it is better, less humiliating, if people don't know you're waiting. Children were ignorant. The strength of adulthood lay in being dignified enough not to expose this impatience. It was worse for women.

That was "Portrait of a Lady". I wrote more, while I waited, and soon had most of the stories for a new book, *World's End*.

At last the man responded. He liked the play, he said, and the more he praised it the deeper my heart sank, because even then I knew that when someone in the movies or the theatre praised you it was death, and "I'm terribly excited about it" is one of the cruellest judgements. Since in that business the most passionate emotion is envy, silence is the most telling response – or else abuse, in which every word means its opposite.

Anyway, this terribly excited man was leaving the country, but in the meantime I could tidy up the script, couldn't I? He had three other plays to direct. That's the other thing. Most of these people are desperately looking for work.

By then I had evaporated in disgust. I went to Honduras and lived on bananas and thought: *This is the life*. And I nerved myself to begin writing *The Mosquito Coast*.

I put *The White Man's Burden* in a drawer. It was not staged. Only now is it seeing the light of day, and for several reasons. I think it is worth preserving. And also this year is an anniversary, my twentieth; my first book appeared in 1967, on my birthday.

My wife Anne made a number of comments after a careful reading of this play. I gladly dedicate it to her, with love, in our own twentieth year.

Paul Theroux
London, 10 April, 1987

INTRODUCTION

Rudyard Kipling: The White Man's Burden

One of the more grotesque falsifications of taste, and it is usually propounded in schools, is the pious belief that a work of literature must be morally pure and right-minded before it can wholly satisfy us. No villain can enthrall us, the argument runs; no sinful passion can make us happy or inspire us. And yet if this were so, half of literature would be lost to us in our self-denying refusal to see, as Angus Wilson puts it in *The Strange Ride of Rudyard Kipling*, "the difficult truth that aesthetic satisfaction is not one with ethical satisfaction". There are morally disgusting stories that one reads with absolute enchantment, and from the Jacobeans onward villains who are truer and vastly more enjoyable than saintly heroes who never put a foot wrong.

Kipling embarrasses critics, and even his biographers have felt the necessity to suppress stories they have found morally untidy or politically dubious. We have had to endure the preposterous suggestions that Kipling wasn't really an imperialist, or vindictive in his fictions, or that he didn't scoff at some races and hate others. But he did believe in the salvation of imperialism, and any number of his stories and poems indicate his hatred for certain races or groups of people. No, not Indians, though he made Kim's companion a Buddhist rather than a Hindu; but apart from his approval of "Fuzzy Wuzzy" in his home in the Sudan he never referred to Africans as other than "Hubshis" (a neat Hindi evasion derived from "Abyssinians") and he believed that the Germans were satanic. These views in fine and subtle works have caused confusion and have made Kipling one of the most misunderstood writers in the language.

Long before he died (he died comparatively recently, in 1936) he was praised, mocked and hounded in about equal measure. After his death he was ignored for a decade, then pounced upon – so vigorously that a book published in 1945, Hilton Brown's *Rudyard Kipling*, proclaims that its intention is for Kipling "to be restored to his throne". Orwell's defensive and indignant essay was mainly a response to Eliot's saying (in his selection of Kipling's poems) that Kipling was "a versifier". In America, Randall Jarrell tried with a certain amount of success to make sure that "the Kipling that nobody read" (the title of Edmund Wilson's essay) reached a wide public. In England, Somerset Maugham edited a companion piece to Eliot's, a selection of stories he prefaced with the view that Kipling was the greatest short story writer in English. More recently, V. S. Naipaul has discussed – but not dismissed – Kipling as "a club writer", and Philip Mason in an enormous book of critical chat (*Kipling: The Glass, the Shadow and the Fire*) has directed our interest to the later stories. Charles Carrington's official biography (it appeared in 1955, but has been reissued with corrections) started a new Kipling boom; it is a politely factual book, plodding and reverential, that goes its earnest way, buffing up the slightly tarnished halo. Both J. I. M. Stewart and Angus Wilson have improved our understanding – Mr Wilson in particular – but some bafflements have persisted.

And no wonder, for Kipling himself was no help. In his lifetime Kipling actively discouraged anyone from invading his privacy. He had a mighty distrust of journalists, and in his poem "The Appeal" he wrote,

> And for the little, little span
>   The dead are borne in mind,
> Seek not to question other than
>   The books I leave behind.

Fine, you say, and you pause at the Kipling shelf. Here it is, nearly as long as The Grand Trunk Road and with much the same motley traffic: kiddies' stories and "Mary Postgate" (one of the nastiest stories ever written), poems about Puck and poems about whores and sergeants, fables about immortality and one disagreeable ode about the Kaiser dying of throat cancer; a great knowingness about adultery and divorce and spooks in cupboards, written when he was in his twenties, and some later stories that are positively boyish. There is the precise technical detail of railway engines and radios, and the hilarious photographic gaffe in "The End of the Passage" where a character snaps a picture of the bogeyman printed on a dead man's retina. He never saw Mandalay, and yet it is the title of his best-known poem; he suffered in America, but wrote remarkably little about it. His India, which has become our India (and even many Indians' India – the scholar Nirad Chaudhuri ranks *Kim* as far greater than Forster's *Passage to India*), he imagined from just seven years of working on colonial newspapers and mooching in Simla and the bazaar. From year to year he is reassessed. He has never, I think, gone unread; but a wilder combination of traits – philistinism and fine-feeling, vulgarity and clear-sightedness, militarism and mercy, public serenity and private sorrow, fierceness and gentleness – is hard to imagine. Could there be a better subject for a novel or play?

This play about Kipling seems to me (but I hope to no one else) like the sort of Chinese pot I have seen reassembled in a museum case. A dozen or so fragments of porcelain, big and small, are dug up; they do not make a whole pot, but a careful man studying the breaks and curves in the pieces begins to fathom the design. With new clay and old fragments he makes his vessel, the plain biscuit-colored clay holding the opaline fragments in place. It is the right shape, but a strange mixture of styles and tones, a work of collaboration, the past informing the present. Sometimes, if it is done well, you hardly notice the patches. In a sense, most writing is like this; the writer is usually working with vivid splinters and trying to make their shine indistinguishable in his creation.

I was lucky in the fragments I found.

The story began in London, in 1889. Kipling was then twenty-four and living in several small rooms on Villiers Street, next to Charing Cross Station. He had made his reputation with his book of short stories, *Plain Tales from the Hills*, and he was regarded as a prodigy. He had recently returned from India; he was hard at work. Not very far away, in Dean's Yard, Westminster, there was an American about Kipling's age, who had just arrived and was energetically writing, signing up authors for a new publishing venture, and moving in society. This was Wolcott Balestier. He was all bustle – charming, impatient, clever, imaginative, business-like. He had already written two novels, but now he had a new scheme.

The American copyright laws allowed any foreign book to be pirates' loot – Dickens had complained about this some years earlier. The only way an English author could secure copyright in the United States was in collaboration with an author who was an American citizen. Soon after he set up his office in Dean's Yard, Wolcott hired Arthur Waugh (Evelyn's father) as his assistant – it was Arthur Waugh's first job. In his autobiography, *One Man's Road* (1931), Waugh wrote that Wolcott had "conceived the idea of crossing to England, and setting up a collaboration with some established English writer, say, Mrs Humphry Ward – which would secure that writer the protection of American copyright".

Waugh was impressed by his young boss. The American was tremendously hard-working and deeply respected. He was, said Waugh, "an inspired leader, and made everybody, or almost everybody, believe in him". Wolcott's motto was that nothing was impossible: you could do anything, meet anyone, go anywhere, change the copyright laws, make a fortune or effect any conquest. "He was not merely one of our conquerers," Edmund Gosse wrote, "but the most successful of them all."

It was almost inevitable that Wolcott should meet Rud-yard Kipling, although the first time he heard of him he said, "Rudyard Kipling – is it a man or a woman? What's its real name?" Very soon Wolcott was discussing the possibility of publishing Kipling in America and – odd for the reclusive and single-minded Englishman – collaborating with him on a novel, to be called *The Naulahka* (the word was misspelled: Kipling never corrected it). Kipling began visiting Wolcott; he met Wolcott's mother and two sisters, who were very proud of the way Wolcott had made inroads on English society. At the same time, Wolcott was cultivating the friendship of Henry James, and to his occupations of publisher, novelist, collaborator, and party-goer he added one more – he became Henry James's literary agent. "The precious Balestier," James called him, and in a letter to a friend he wrote, "He will probably strike you, as he strikes me, as the perfection of an 'agent'." James was then fifty. He treated Wolcott as his son, and they made trips together – once, they planned to spend a weekend on the Isle of Wight, but it was more than a week before the pair returned to London. "He became in a manner part of my life," James wrote. There can be no doubt that James loved him in the helplessly idealizing way that he did attractive and talented young men.

Henry James also met Wolcott's sisters. Josephine was very pretty, and perhaps as a consequence of her unapproachable beauty we know almost nothing about her. Caroline, known to everyone as "Carrie", was "a little person of extraordinary capacity", James said. She was small and genial, and capable to the point where a number of people compared her to a man. Kipling's parents were slightly alarmed by her. His father remarked obliquely that she was "a good man spoiled", and his over-protective mother said, "That woman is going to marry our Ruddy."

It is not known what sort of courtship, if any, went on between Carrie and Kipling. The focus of attention was Wolcott, who was now doing business in Europe. He had joined forces with the English firm of Heinemann in the hope of producing cheap pocket editions of novels, to rival those of Tauchnitz. Kipling meanwhile set off alone, in a state of mental exhaustion brought on by overwork, for a round-the-world cruise. He visited South Africa and New Zealand, and he had given Henry James the impression that he was on his way to Samoa to visit Robert Louis Stevenson. Indeed, Stevenson expected him: "R. K. is planning to visit us," he wrote to James in September, 1891. But Kipling abandoned the Samoa trip and sailed to Australia and Ceylon. In Colombo he had news that Wolcott was dangerously ill; just before Christmas in Lahore he learned the Wolcott had died in early December, in Dresden.

Henry James had been summoned to Dresden. He dreaded the errand, but managed to play a fatherly role at the bleak funeral ceremony. James was desolated by Wolcott's death, but full of admiration for Carrie's fortitude, "the intense – and almost manly – nature of her emotion". The Balestier women and James returned to England, and they were astonished to see Kipling on the 10th of January – it had taken him just fourteen days to travel from Bombay to London. A week later, Kipling and Carrie were married, at All Souls, Langham Place. Henry James gave the bride away – "a queer office for *me* to perform – but it's done – and an odd little marriage".

A month after their marriage, in the middle of February, 1892, the Kiplings were in America. They stopped at Brattleboro, Vermont, where some of Carrie's relatives lived, and Kipling was overwhelmed by the snow and the isolation. With the haste that characterized his decisions during this first hectic part of his life, Kipling determined to buy some land, build a house and live in Vermont. All this he managed quickly, and then the honeymoon couple crossed America to Vancouver, sailed to Japan (where Carrie's maternal grandfather had been an adviser, twenty years earlier, to the Mikado) and discovered, one afternoon in Yokohama, that their bank had gone bust. Penniless, they returned to Brattleboro. That story is in Kipling's somewhat evasive autobiography, *Something of Myself*, written when he was seventy.

No reader of this autobiography can have much idea of what Kipling's American years were like. You get the impression that he has a grievance, but it is impossible to say how it came about. The book is short on particulars – unusual for a writer who could describe down to the last valve and piston ring the workings of a steam engine. But perhaps that was the problem. James described Kipling's writing as a steady diminishing, moving from "the less simple in subject to the more simple – from the Anglo-Indians to the natives, from the natives to the Tommies, from the Tommies to the quadrupeds, from the quadrupeds to the fish and from the fish to the engines and screws". There is no mention in Kipling's autobiography of the vast amount of work he did in Brattleboro (he doesn't even name the town), but the four years after his marriage – Kipling was filled with optimism and settled for the first time in his life – were the most productive of his literary career. He wrote most of the poems in *The Seven Seas*, both *Jungle Books*, all the stories in *The Day's Work*, the second series of *Barrack-Room Ballads*, worked at *Mother Maturin* (he was never happy with this novel and finally ditched it), started *Kim* and wrote most of *Captains Courageous* – this last was his only strictly American book. He also wrote a number of poems which were subsequently collected. His output was enormous and profitable and within a few years the Yokohama bankruptcy became no more than a funny incident, part of the colorful past.

Kipling loved the American landscape; he was uncertain of the people. He hated the drinking, the talking, the spitting, the greed, the noise, the illiterate immigrants, the xenophobia – specifically a hurtful anti-British feeling which prevailed in the 1890s. "So far as I was concerned," he wrote in *Something of Myself*, "I felt the atmosphere was to some extent hostile. The idea seemed to be that I was 'making money' out of America – witness the new house and the horses – and was not sufficiently grateful for my privileges."

There is no reference in his autobiography to his brother-in-law, Beatty Balestier, or to the Venezuela-British Guiana boundary dispute which brought America and Britain to the brink of war. The Beatty memory must have been horrible – no human being could have been less like Kipling in character than Beatty. It is not surprising that the two men fought. I am inclined to think that Kipling identified in Beatty all the weaknesses and evils he saw in the United States: Beatty, for him, was the very embodiment of the boasting, irresponsible American. And it is quite likely that Beatty saw in Kipling a young John Bull, imperious, aloof, dedicated to work, unfunny and not particularly friendly. We know Beatty from his shouts of pain and pleasure; he was not immoral, only extravagant, coarsely expressive and loud, with the harum-scarum attitude of Huck Finn. He had Wolcott's energetic presumption, but none of Wolcott's tact or grace. Beatty was popular in town; Kipling was not and, what was worse, Kipling did not give a damn. But when Kipling decided to take on Beatty – breaking all his own rules about settling arguments in a judiciously wolf-like way – he did not know how it would expose and humiliate him, and how it would drive him out of his first real home.

Kipling placed much of the blame for the anti-British feeling in America on the national press. From his first visit to the States he was appalled by the state of American newspapers, and it was not long before he was pestered by journalists. He was usually successful at keeping them at bay, but his evasions only convinced them that he would make good copy. They hounded him as he disembarked from ships, they sneaked onto his property, interviewed neighbors and generally made a nuisance of themselves. Kipling never changed his view that the journalists were bums and their papers foolish, trivial and jingoistic. In doing research for my play, I read many American newspapers published in 1895 and 1896 and, with some regret – the *Boston Post* was one of the most scabrous of the bunch – I began to see Kipling's point. The front pages were filled with reports of murders, muggings, suicides, gossip, hearsay, "society" rubbish and tub-thumping over Cuba and Venezuela. Kipling saw these same papers. He could have ignored them; he could have dismissed Beatty's ravings as wild talk – it wasn't much more than that. But in the end he brought the journalists to his doorstep and the scorn of the press upon his head. Rashly, in May, 1896, he had Beatty arrested.

I think he was striking the blow he believed Lord Salisbury should have struck a few months before. Britain had been taunted over the boundary between Venezuela and British Guiana – Venezuela making the ridiculous claim that well over half the British colony was rightfully her own. This issue had been in the air for about fifty years, but in 1895 the Venezuelans jumped a part of the disputed territory, captured an outpost and fired on a British schooner. When Lord Salisbury demanded their withdrawal, the United States asserted the Monroe Doctrine. Secretary of State Olney provided a clumsy gloss on the Monroe Doctrine by telling Lord Salisbury that "Distance and three thousand miles of intervening ocean make any permanent political union between a European and an American state unnatural and inexpedient." (Some years later, Olney explained his sharp tone by saying that "in English eyes the United States was then so completely a negligible quantity that it was believed only words the equivalent of blows would be really effective".) Olney's message was delivered in July; it was not until November that Lord Salisbury replied. To Olney's charge that union between Britain and British Guiana was "unnatural and inexpedient", Lord Salisbury said, "Her Majesty's Government are prepared emphatically to deny it on behalf of both British and American people who are subject to her Crown." He went on,

> Great Britain is imposing no "system" upon Venezuela . . . It is a controversy with which the United States have no apparent concern . . . It is not a question of the imposition upon the communities of South America of any system of government devised in Europe. It is simply the determination of the frontier of a British possession which belonged to the Throne of England long before the Republic of Venezuela came into existence.

Lord Salisbury called the Monroe Doctrine "a novelty" and said it was not recognized as any part of international law. He implied that he would deal with the Venezuelans in his own way.

This was fierce, but the American response to it was so threatening that it produced panic on Wall Street and an uprush of reckless patriotism that was given voice in anti-British sentiment. The American reply was President Cleveland's Message to Congress of 17 December, 1895. He said that, as Britain had refused to submit the boundary question to arbitration, he would request that Congress set up a commission to determine the true Venezuela-British Guiana frontier. In closing, he said,

> When such report is made and accepted it will in my opinion be the duty of the United States to resist by every means in its power as a willful aggression upon its rights and interests the appropriation of Great Britain of any lands or the exercise of governmental jurisdiction over any territory which after investigation we have determined of right belongs to Venezuela.

In making these recommendations I am fully alive to the

responsibility incurred and keenly realize all the consequences that may follow.

I am nevertheless firm in my conviction that while it is a grievous thing to contemplate the two great English-speaking peoples of the world as being otherwise than friendly competitors in the onward march of civilization, and strenuous and worthy rivals in all the arts of peace, there is no calamity which a great nation can invite which equals that which follows a supine submission to wrong and injustice and the consequent loss of national self-respect and honor beneath which are shielded and defended a people's safety and greatness.

Even gracelessly under-punctuated, Cleveland's message was clear: We will fight you if you don't accept our commission's decision.

In his *Oxford History of the United States*, Samuel Eliot Morison interprets the provocative language as growing out of a suspicion that the British government was procrastinating and that Venezuela, "if further put off, would declare a war, in which the United States must participate". It is true, as Lord Salisbury's biographer said of him, that he could be masterfully inactive, but Morison's is a charitable assessment, a historian's retrospective look at a bewildering piece of intransigence by two great powers over a precinct of South American jungle. Still, it gladdened Americans and it encouraged Latin Americans – the dictator, Porfirio Díaz, crowed his approval in Mexico City (but it was not long before he would be fleeing to safety in Europe). Seeing that the atmosphere had become hostile, Kipling wondered whether he might not be better off in Canada. He wrote hysterically to his friends, with his hopeless reading of the situation. He and his coachman were the only Englishmen in Brattleboro: the "little wooden town, white-cloaked and dumb" had become enemy territory.

For Henry James, still gloomy over the failure of his disastrous stage play, *Guy Domville*, the American belligerence was cause for greater gloom. He compared Cleveland's outburst of militarism to something Bismarck might utter in Germany. He expressed his fears in a letter to his brother, William:

One must hope that sanity and civilization, in both countries, will prevail. But the lurid light the American newspapers seem to project on the quantity of resident Anglophobia in the U.S. – the absolute war-hunger as against this country – is a thing to darken one's meditations. When, why does it, today, explode in such immense volume – in such apparent preponderance, and whither does it tend? It stupefies me – seems to me horribly inferior and vulgar – and I shall never go with it . . . I had rather my bones were ground into British powder!

Henry James was ashamed and angry in London. In Brattleboro Kipling was frenzied, and he saw that it might be impossible for him to continue living in this small provincial town.

When the British government finally capitulated, in a face-saving gesture of agreeing to a treaty with Venezuela for submission of the dispute to arbitration, they did so because they were afraid of Germany, rather than out of any apprehension over an American attack. In the early winter of 1896, the German Kaiser had sent a telegram of congratulation to President Kruger of the Transvaal after the Boers frustrated the Jameson raid. It was clear to the British that a war in South Africa was imminent. This also had the effect of chastening what Joseph Pulitzer called the "jingo bugaboo" of President Cleveland. But none of this was any comfort to Kipling, who saw his leonine government provoked from another part of the globe.

It was at this time, from the first rumblings over Venezuela, to a British defeat (with German applause) in South Africa, that Kipling quarrelled with Beatty Balestier, had him arrested on a charge of "threatening murder and assault with opprobrious language", participated in the Brattleboro hearing, and made his decision to leave the United States for good. These unusual events – unusual for Kipling, at any rate – are the subject of my play.

A Grand Jury trial was set for September, but the day after the May hearing the newspapers – which had made a meal of it – carried headlines to the effect that Kipling was leaving. *Goodbye, Green Mountains!* and *The Author, After a Day as Witness, Says He's "Sick of the Whole Business"* were the headlines in the *New York Herald*; and the *New York Times*'s was *Kipling Talks of Leaving the Country to Protect Himself*. The local Brattleboro paper the *Phoenix*, carried no mention of Kipling's plan to leave, and indeed reported the hearing with dignity and impartiality. In an editorial published three days after the hearing, the paper gave Kipling's knuckles a gentle rap: "For reasons which Mr Kipling doubtless knows very well, the reporters have seen here a chance to get even with him." The editorial went on to summarize his behavior:

> He has chosen to live his life in his own way, and the Brattleboro community have respected his reserve. Whatever rebuffs ambitious interviewers from the city press may have invited, Mr Kipling's townsfolk have given themselves no occasion for grievance in this respect. He has undertaken no social responsibilities and has made few personal friends, but these few have found him the most genial and delightful of men. What seems to us his unfortunate way of meeting the well-meant advances of newspaper men and would-be friends of the literary guild when he first came to this country won him a reputation for exceeding brusqueness, and, in the public mind this covered and sunk out of sight the sensitive, appreciative and intense temperament which intimate friends know him to possess, and the mark of which is found on all his best work.

It was blame and praise. It ended with a cordial invitation for Kipling to stay, and the hope that Brattleboro would "long be his home". Kipling did not reply to this; if he commented privately no record survives.

The next newspaper report of Kipling is an item from the *Boston Journal* (22 May, 1896) about another visit by him to Gloucester "to afford him material for the story of New England life upon which he is now at work". Two months later, the *Phoenix* reported that *Captains Courageous* was nearly done and that the serial rights had been sold to McClure's magazine. At the end of July there was a tiny paragraph in the *Phoenix* about Kipling planning to build "an additional farm barn" (and under this, "Austin Miller has placed a pop corn and peanut roaster in front of his store"). On the evidence of these newspaper stories it seemed as if Kipling was planning to stay in town for the September trial, and perhaps much longer. The trial was now only a month away.

But the *New York Times* of September 2nd carried a small report on an inside page which settled the question. The headline was *Rudyard Kipling Goes Abroad*:

> Rudyard Kipling, the novelist, accompanied by his wife and children, sailed yesterday on the North German Lloyd Steamship *Lahn* for Southampton. Mr Kipling will be gone for several years. He goes direct to Torquay, a small fishing village situated in the south of England. Although he has removed all his furniture from his home in Naulakha, Vt., he did not take it with him, but stored it in Rutland, Vt.

Apparently, Kipling told the New York reporters, "I expect to come back when I get ready. I haven't the least idea when that will be."

Three years later, in 1899, Kipling returned to New York, intending to make a visit to Brattleboro. But he fell ill with pneumonia and for many days he was near to death. His small daughter Josephine was also dangerously ill. The papers reported that Beatty Balestier had hurried to New York to bring a court action against Kipling, demanding $50,000 damages for "malicious persecution, false arrest and defamation of character". Within days, little Josephine died; this terrible news was kept from Kipling until he recovered. Sick with grief, he took the remainder of his family away from the United States – without making the one-day journey to Vermont – and he never returned. Forty years later, Beatty was still talking about his old enemy. "He never has come back to Vermont," he said to one writer. "He never will, while I'm alive."

So Kipling stayed in England. After a few years he found a large isolated house in Sussex. He was just thirty-seven, but already he seemed to the world, and to his family, an old man. The American experience – the shock in Brattleboro, the death of his daughter in New York – had aged and saddened him. He said he had "discovered England" and "at last, I'm one of the gentry". He lived in this house for the rest of his life, and he did not write about America until, at the age of seventy, he described it in his autobiography. He seemed embittered, and people wondered why. An American friend wrote to inquire. Kipling replied, "Remember that I lived in that land for four years as a householder . . . As the nigger said in Court: 'If I didn't like de woman, how come I take de trouble to hit her on de haid?'"

ACT ONE

ACT ONE

Scene 1

It is a snowy December at Naulakha, Rudyard Kipling's home in Vermont. The year is 1895.

At the center-rear of the stage is a large fireplace, on which is inscribed in large letters (from John 9:14) "THE NIGHT COMETH WHEN NO MAN CAN WORK". There are some bookcases, but the walls are indefinite. There is a sofa and some chairs. Later, when the lights come up we will see a pair of skis and some golf clubs standing against a bookcase. On the mantelpiece is a bronze statuette of a wolf. There is a newspaper on a small chairside table.

This is Kipling's study, but it is also in a sense his mind. With small changes it is the only set in the play. Ideally, it is a space surrounded by darkness. From time to time characters invade it, confront Kipling and then vanish. It is his American privacy, but it is not private.

When the play opens only Kipling's desk is lit – by a lamp. The desk, very large, is in front of the fireplace. Kipling sits at the desk. He smokes a pipe and is dressed in a tweed jacket and plus-fours. He has thick eyebrows, his hair is cut short, his mustache is full and fierce. He is quite near-sighted and wears pebble glasses. He gives the impression of intense energy, and it is only when he stands that he is revealed as small and wiry. He is famous in every part of the world, except Brattleboro, Vermont, where he is regarded as stand-offish and a bit high-falutin. He is only thirty-one, but his manner – by turns imperious, impish, ironical, and sometimes bluntly angry – has done little to reassure the townsfolk.

3

His public attitude is one of almost military correct-
ness, but privately he talks in a pleasingly off-hand way.
He writes, stops, and inclines his head as if listening. He
shakes his head.

KIPLING: Never!

He listens again. Looks at the newspaper. He
smiles.

Never! because *Allahu-akhbar*. I was in San
Francisco. Once. And I saw with great joy that
the blockhouse which guards (*American accent*)
"the finest harbor in the world, sir" could be
silenced by two gunboats from Hong Kong, with
safety and dispatch. (*Pause*) New York would be
easier.

We could take it before breakfast – take it back!

He rises and moves toward the newspaper.

Washington? (*Mockingly*) A colossal agglom-
eration reeking bounders! We'd give 'em
corkscrews and brush-drill! (*Pause*)

Brattleboro, Vermont? Dishwater! We'd fix 'em
with ag-ags and head-knuckles.

As he speaks he carries the newspaper to the desk
and, still standing, flattens it on the desk and
reads it, hovering over it. It is the posture of a
man who has spent some time in a newspaper
office. He takes his pen and marks paragraphs.
*   Kipling is absorbed. We then hear an Amer-*
ican voice, from stage-right. It is that of Beatty
Balestier, Kipling's brother-in-law.

BEATTY: Distance and three thousand miles of intervening
ocean make any permanent political union between a European and American state unnatural
and inexpedient.

Kipling does not look up, though the speech has

4

been delivered in an orotund way, with a political tub-thumper's emphasis.

KIPLING: For "European" read "British". For "American state" read "Venezuela".

BEATTY: The disputed frontier of British Guiana and Venezuela will be determined by a report made by a Congressional commission.

KIPLING: British Guiana belonged to the Throne of England long before the Republic of Venezuela came into existence. Before the American Rebellion, or the United States, or Grover Cleveland, for that matter!

Beatty has emerged from the darkness into the study. He goes to a shelf, takes a decanter of sherry and pours himself a drink. Seemingly angered by what Kipling has just said, he speaks with fury.

BEATTY: When such report is made and accepted it will in my opinion be the duty of the United States to resist *by every means in its power*, as a willful aggression upon its rights and interests, the appropriation of Great Britain of any lands, or the exercise of governmental jurisdiction over any territory, which after investigation we have determined of right belongs to Venezuela.

KIPLING: (*still reading, thumps the paper and shouts*) War!

BEATTY: I am fully alive to the responsibility incurred and keenly realize all the consequences that may follow.

KIPLING: (*smiling slightly*) Two gun-boats from Hong Kong. Head-knuckles.

BEATTY: I am nevertheless firm in my conviction that, while it is a grievous thing to contemplate the two great English-speaking peoples of the world

5

as being otherwise than friendly competitors in the onward march of civilization, there is no calamity which a great nation can invite which equals that which –

Stops speechifying, pours himself another drink, sips and continues.

KIPLING: (*sarcastically*) *English*-speaking peoples!

BEATTY: Which equals that which follows a supine submission to wrong and injustice –

Sips the sherry between each pompous phrase.

– and the consequent loss of national self-respect and honor beneath which are shielded and defended a people's safety and greatness.

Kipling does not address Beatty directly in the following dialogue – rather, he talks past him. Nevertheless he is keenly aware of his presence and is occasionally threatened by it.

(*sharply*) Venezuela is American.

KIPLING: Guiana is British, and has been since Raleigh. She doesn't pay her way, but she's got a government and laws and she's not the grease-spot that Venezuela is. A lot of white men died in Guiana to keep her alive.

BEATTY: They smelled the gold of Eldorado. Money's the only reason for colonies. When there isn't a virgin or a dollar left, the white men go.

KIPLING: The Venezuelans have jumped the border, laid claim to British territory, captured an outpost and fired on a British schooner. We demanded your withdrawal – and your response to this? You've sided with these Venezuelan pirates! What earthly right do you have to interfere in the affairs of these sovereign countries?

BEATTY: It's all spelled out in the Monroe Doctrine. I'll have my Secretary of State send you a copy.

KIPLING: Keep it. It has no place in international law. Just another piece of Yankee pomp.

BEATTY: We are the law on this continent.

KIPLING: Which continent?

BEATTY: From Eskimo-land to Cape Horn. Don't tread on us.

Beatty has started to leave, backing into the darkness.

KIPLING: We will educate you as we see fit.

BEATTY: (*in farewell*) Go home! (*he leaves*)

KIPLING: I *am* home! I found this town, I built this house, I'll never leave.

As Kipling returns to his newspaper, there are voices, stage-left: Carrie Kipling's and Matthew Howard's.

CARRIE: What is it?

HOWARD: I'm sorry, but it's dead urgent, Madam –

CARRIE: You know Mr. Kipling is not to be disturbed –

KIPLING: (*brightly*) Bring him in – I'm done messing with ink, my dear.

We see Carrie first. She goes over to Kipling. She is older than Kipling by almost four years and is heavily pregnant with her second child.

    Matthew enters breathlessly. This is Kipling's coachman. He is smartly dressed in twill trousers and a frock coat. He has become Kipling's right-hand man – very efficient and very loyal.

Matthew, you're blue and white! Have you been out in this blizzard?

HOWARD: Yes, sir. Sorry to be a flaming nuisance, sir. But I was down clearing snow off the path, and –

7

KIPLING: Dressed in that kit? I ask you, Carrie. Isn't that a lesson to the aborigines?

HOWARD: I tries, sir. I was saying – I was down the path and seen a lady. I takes up my broom, and I seen her, sir, perishing with cold.

KIPLING: What would a lady be doing, strolling round Naulakha in a blizzard like this?

HOWARD: She weren't strollin', sir, She were mired-up in it. Her hands was froze, and her boots was soaked through.

KIPLING: You didn't leave her out there, I trust.

HOWARD: I was going to take her down to Maplewood or Waite's Corner, but the cold had got to her, and the snow was 'eaving down. I know you don't want strangers 'ere, but (to Carrie), Madam, I done the only thing I could do. There wasn't anything for it but for me to take her in, and carry her at that. She's in the kitchen, sir. My Mabel's seein' to her. I thought you ought to know. I'm sorry for interferin' –

KIPLING: You did the right thing –

CARRIE: What sort of lady? Is she respectable?

HOWARD: It's so hard to tell in this country. She's not a common sort. The hat was proper. And she's not local.

CARRIE: How do you know that?

HOWARD: The locals know better than to come up here.

KIPLING: Perhaps you'd be good enough to see to her, my dear. (He thinks again) No – show her in here, Matthew. We're not savages, in spite of what our kind neighbors think. I shan't keep waifs and strays in my kitchen. It's a rum sort of lady who takes these blizzardy hills for an esplanade! She must have pluck! Fetch her, Matthew, and we'll see what the storm has brought us.

8

HOWARD: Very good, sir. (*He leaves*)

CARRIE: But you're busy, Rud.

KIPLING: I'm curious.

CARRIE: A strange woman, gallivanting about after dark in a blizzard. Heaven knows how she got here.

KIPLING: Lost her way – compass all askew – snowshoes sprung a leak.

CARRIE: I'll have a fire lit in the lounge. (*Pause*)

           I had hoped to have a talk with Beatty tonight. He was here this afternoon while I was out.

KIPLING: Now there's someone who deserves to be left in a snowbank. No, I haven't laid eyes on that American for weeks.

CARRIE: He left word that he'd be back. I can put our idea to him.

KIPLING: It could be the making of him – if he stopped pickling himself in alcohol.

CARRIE: I think I should talk to Beatty alone. He's so uneasy with you.

KIPLING: Is that uneasiness? Why I could have sworn it was bloody-mindedness or cheek or something awfuller. Now if he'd been in the army they would have treated him like the heathen he is.

CARRIE: He's still a boy.

KIPLING: With a wife and child and the debts of a viceroy – hardly a boy, just an unfinished man. No, I don't mind carrying him by the slack of his breeches if it does some good, don't you know. But I refuse to be a patron to the sort of artist whose art is whooping and hollering on a bellyful of –

           Matthew ushers Mary in. Kipling's anger immediately ceases.

           Ah – the wanderer!

9

Mary is very pretty, but clearly suffering the effects of her ordeal in the snow. She is well-dressed but bedraggled; dazed and grateful, still thawing. She carries a large leather bag. From time to time she reaches into it, pulls out a hanky and sneezes.

KIPLING: Over here, my dear, near the fire. Bring another chair, Matthew. Why this is a great surprise – we haven't rescued anyone from the snow for some time. But you've come through admirably. Here, sit down.

MARY: Thank you. (*She sits*) You're so kind.

HOWARD: Will that be all, sir?

KIPLING: Excellent, thank you, Matthew.

Matthew leaves the room.

MARY: I think I frightened that man.

CARRIE: I doubt it. Matthew doesn't scare easily.

MARY: I was just lying there in the snow. He didn't seem to know what to do.

CARRIE: He has orders to turn strangers away. The grounds are posted.

MARY: Maybe that was it. Gee, I couldn't understand a single word he said. What is he – Scotch? I didn't see any signs.

KIPLING: They're only five feet high – I expect they're buried. We'll see them again in May or thereabouts. We'd put up fences but it's not considered neighborly, don't you know. So my wife had No Trespassing signs put up. But even that was a compromise.

MARY: In what way?

KIPLING: I suggested *No Hawkers* and hers was *Trespassers Will Be Shot.*

10

MARY: I'm glad that Scotchman didn't shoot me! But I
            was feeling really unlucky all the same. I wasn't
            expecting snow like this!

CARRIE: You're from – ?

MARY: Boston. This fire is wonderful. What a lovely
            fireplace. "The Night Cometh When No Man
            Can Work" – that's pretty.

KIPLING: Scripture. "I must work the works of him that
            sent me while it is day" et cetera.

CARRIE: But it snows in Boston, surely?

MARY: They shovel it in Boston. I got real worried out
            there. I couldn't move I was so cold.

CARRIE: (to Kipling) We should get those signs posted a
            bit higher where they can be seen.

KIPLING: (to Mary) You'll be all right here – you go ahead
            and thaw out. Have you eaten?

MARY: Lunch.

KIPLING: Carrie, perhaps cook has some soup left – that'll
            kindle some warmth in this young lady. (To
            Mary) I'm frightfully sorry – my name is Kipling.

MARY: (impressed) I'm honored, Mr. Kipling, believe
            me I am really –

KIPLING: And this is Mrs. Kipling, You have arrived at
            Naulakha.

MARY: They told me it was Waite's Corner.

KIPLING: Four Corners is down the road – that's Waite's
            farm and the post office. This house is Naulakha.

MARY: Sounds Indian.

KIPLING: Not your sort of Redskin Indian, but Indian all
            the same. It's a number – nine lakhs, nine
            hundred thousand.

MARY: That's some street address!

11

CARRIE: And you are?

MARY: Mary Hackett.

KIPLING: Hackett. Irish?

MARY: Yes, both sides of the family. My mother's an O'Brien. One of the Roxbury O'Briens.

KIPLING: (*mock-interest*) One of the Roxbury O'Briens.

CARRIE: I'll see to the soup. It will be served in the dining-room.

Carrie goes out.

MARY: I feel better already. I want you to know that I'm very sorry about this, Mr. Kipling.

KIPLING: Don't think about it. Make yourself at home. To tell you the truth, I was getting a bit bored. You can count yourself an early Christmas visitor.

MARY: It's going to be a white Christmas, that's for sure.

KIPLING: You know what you want in snow like this? (*He walks to the skis which are propped near the fireplace*) Know what they are?

MARY: I don't know – maybe bean poles!

KIPLING: Skis.

MARY: I've heard about them.

KIPLING: This is the only pair in Vermont – maybe the only pair in the United States of America.

MARY: Gosh, where'd you get them?

KIPLING: These were a present – given to me by Arthur Conan Doyle.

MARY: The detective?

KIPLING: That's right. He got them in Austria. He was over here last year and thought I needed them. You want to get yourself a pair.

MARY: You think it'd be proper?

12

KIPLING: Rather. It's a lovely game – skiing. Just the thing for an American girl. Of course you'll need some lessons, but you need lessons with anything, even cycling.

MARY: Have you got a cycle, too?

KIPLING: I have a wheel, yes. I took some lessons in New York this year, at that cycling school near the park.

MARY: They say it's the most fashionable cycling school in the world.

KIPLING: We took some rather unfashionable spills, don't you know. There were an awful lot of American girls there. You have good times, I must say. You travel and get about. You have freedom and you're clever enough not to abuse it. I admire that.

MARY: It's nice of you to say. Maybe I'll get me some skis. I can ski down Beacon Hill.

KIPLING: That'll start the town talking! But don't you mind what people say. They'll say anything. If the people around here took up skiing, instead of spending their time drinking and talking in that furtive and false way, this would be the happy place it deserves to be. They worry about the snow. They stay indoors from November to May and do nothing but get frowstier and frowstier. But the snow is magic – magic. People in India spend weeks making a *yatra* from the plains to the hills just for a glimpse of it. Some years it falls on Simla, to general rejoicing. Look at it – how could it not come from heaven? But does your Vermonter appreciate it? No, Miss Hackett, he's a Green Mountain boy – summer and cider, that's what he hankers for. His heaven is easily made – a jug of apple-jack and a spittoon.

MARY: (*seeing the golf clubs*) I see you play golf.

13

KIPLING: Oh, golf is larks.

MARY: We play it, too. In Boston.

KIPLING: In the summer.

MARY: Yes. Out in Chestnut Hill and Cambridge. Boston's got lots of golf links.

KIPLING: We play in the winter.

MARY: No!

KIPLING: A little imagination, a little tinkering, and you can for anything you like.

MARY: But in the snow? You'd sink down.

KIPLING: We wear snow-shoes.

MARY: You'd lose the ball.

KIPLING: (*takes a ball out of the golf bag*) We don't lose these in the snow.

MARY: A red golf ball! God!

KIPLING: You've got a great country. (*With emphasis*) All you've got to do is learn how to use it right.

MARY: We don't do so bad.

KIPLING: (*explaining in a half-humorous way, not angry*) That, my dear, is a matter of opinion. I wouldn't have thought turning New York City into a glorified pig-trough was using it very well. I suppose there's a reason, but I can't help feeling it's an awfully swinish reason. And the point about a pig-trough is – the bigger it gets, the muckier it is. The more pigs it attracts. And then what have you got? Lawlessness, spitting, boasting and impertinence. That cycling school – they used to have the students cycling in the park, but they had to stop that. You'd never guess why. People used to pelt things at the riders, spit at them, knock them off their wheels. That's gentle, isn't it? The kind souls would tag along and oink

14

	ditties. So the school had to build a private hippodrome to keep these inquisitive and sympathetic New Yorkers out.
MARY:	Is London any better?
KIPLING:	I sometimes think so. But I have no particular fondness for that city either.
MARY:	I've always wanted to go there.
KIPLING:	I'm sure you will, some day. American girls seem to have the knack of getting what they want. And yet you surprise me. The rest of your fellow-countrymen speak of seeing Britain from the bridge of a gun-boat. Why just today your president was delicately referring to us as aggressors.
MARY:	You mean this Venezuela business.
KIPLING:	The British Guiana business.
MARY:	They say there's gold on that border.
KIPLING:	Coconuts more likely, but whatever, it is no business of the United States government. The matter is entirely between Britain and Venezuela. That border has been under discussion for fifty years.
MARY:	Venezuela's helpless – she's appealed to us.
KIPLING:	She'll produce another Bolivar, if the situation warrants. She's capable of it. She's not a subject of the United States – she's a free and independent republic. She – but, my, you are a well-informed young lady.
MARY:	I read the newspapers.
KIPLING:	This hasn't been in the fashion pages.
MARY:	I read all the pages.
KIPLING:	That is a drug I do not recommend to the young.

MARY: I think President Cleveland wants a party issue that people can unite behind. Ninety-six is an election year!

KIPLING: The American war-cry. I'm curious to know how many voters he intends to kill. But you have no vote, so don't deceive yourself. The issue is less complicated than that. It's not gold, it's not coconuts, it's not the Venezuelans, it's not even next year's American election. I would like you to know that I am being impartial when I say that at the bottom of this horrible war-cry is a deep hatred of England –

MARY: (*protesting*) Honestly, I don't see that –

KIPLING: I know a chap – one of the few men in Washington with two sides to his head. We were talking about this very thing and he was a bit surprised that I should wonder at the issue myself. He laughed. He said, "America's hatred of England is the hoop round the staves of the union." It was only later I thought – what an empty barrel the union must be.

MARY: We're a world power, too –

KIPLING: You don't prove you're a world power by starting a pretty little war in a British colony. You do it by governing yourselves with dignity. But, no, John Hay said, "When a man comes up out of the sea we say to him, 'See that big bully over there in the East? That's England. Hate him and you're a good American.'"

MARY: It's possible that a lot of people think that. I don't.

KIPLING: Good for you.

MARY: But we can't help it if we've got a fighting spirit.

KIPLING: The Irish?

MARY: The Americans.

KIPLING: After four years in your country I'm still not sure what an American is. I meet Germans in Pennsylvania – Germans. They count themselves full-blooded Americans and look down gutterally on what they call "foreign trash". I suppose they are referring to me. After all, I am not a German. There is the inrush, the wreckage from Eastern Europe, and your own people, Miss Hackett. You describe yourself as Irish and I take you as such. You aver that you're an American, and I must agree with everyone else – the foreign elements will be assimilated. But most people don't care about that – they're too busy making or losing money. It will make an odd sort of army to face us when the day comes. And it seems the day is not far off.

MARY: If it comes to war I know which side I'll be on.

KIPLING: No, you'll be home, cooking, cleaning, counting the dead from the reports in the newspapers, riding the tram-cars and attending to domestic details. Having your children's boots repaired. You'll be allowed the luxury of picnics and you'll hardly believe that under the same blue sky men can be skirmishing and yelling themselves hoarse. It won't be what you think. And who have you fought? The Mexicans, the eskimos, the redskins. You fought each other.

MARY: We fought you and won.

KIPLING: *You* didn't fight us. The people who fought us in the American rebellion are all dead. Abraham Lincoln killed them all in the Civil War. The next war won't be what you think. Allah is merciful.

Matthew appears somewhat agitated.

HOWARD: Excuse me, sir.

KIPLING: What is it, Matthew?

17

HOWARD: A horse, sir. Round back. I found it tied to one of the birches. I couldn't find Mrs. Kipling.

KIPLING: She's in the kitchen. But don't trouble her with this. Did you recognize the horse?

HOWARD: I was coming to that, sir. I reckon it's one of Mr. Balestier's greys.

KIPLING: It's just like him to sneak up on us.

Kipling turns to Mary.

I'll be right back. We can continue our chat. You mustn't mind me – I shan't mind you. Help yourself to books.

Kipling leaves with Matthew. Mary goes to a shelf, picks out a book, flips through it, puts it back. She looks again, then strays to the desk and begins reading from the paper left lying there. She shows more than usual curiosity. She rests her notebook on the desk and begins making notes.

   While she stands with her back to the door, Beatty Balestier enters. He smiles when he sees Mary. He approaches her. She does not hear him.

BEATTY: Applesauce!

MARY: (*startled*) Oh! You frightened me!

BEATTY: (*sizing her up*) Now who might you be?

MARY: Mary Hackett. (*Darts away from the desk leaving the notebook; catches her breath*) You really did scare me.

BEATTY: Doing a little work?

MARY: (*guiltily*) What do you mean? I was only –

BEATTY: Just joking, don't get het up. Where are you from?

MARY: Boston.

18

BEATTY: People say there are pretty girls in Boston. I used to say that was hogwash. I guess I believe them now.

MARY: That is gallant of you.

BEATTY: Something tells me you don't belong here. You're too pretty. (*Mary doesn't respond*) How do you like staying in this house? They'll bore your pants off.

MARY: I'm not staying here. I was, um, wandering around and got lost. On the road out there. In the snow. They fetched me out.

BEATTY: Why didn't you holler? I would have come and rescued you. I would have lit into that road just as tight as I could jump.

MARY: That's very kind of you.

BEATTY: But that's a hell of thing to be doing – wandering around here.

MARY: I was headed here.

BEATTY: Did they invite you?

MARY: Not exactly, In the end, yes. You ask a lot of questions, Mr. –

BEATTY: Call me Beatty.

MARY: Do you live here in Naulakha?

BEATTY: I wouldn't live in this place for fifty thousand dollars.

MARY: That's a nice round figure.

BEATTY: Like yours. That's what it cost to build. Know how I know? Cause I built it – a dozen Canucks and me, back in '93. We offered him cherry, he wanted ash. Cherry's the same price but it's twice as good. But he knows what he wants – he's an authority on houses. He's an authority on every-thing. British. They don't even make houses out

19

of wood there. But he knows his mind – ash. Made an ash of himself. Know what I call him? Rudyard? The Redcoat!

MARY: That's not very nice.

BEATTY: He calls me worse. Not to my face. But I hear everything. Why, if that man farted in White River Junction I'd hear him in Brattleboro and say, "Catch that fart and paint it red!" Drink?

Beatty goes to the decanter on the shelf, pours himself a drink, offers one to Mary. She shakes her head – no.

This is really my house. Most of the wood's mine. All the labor. The Redcoat was down the road at Bliss Cottage – scribbling, squinting at us. Tried to talk French to the Canucks. Think they understood? Not a word. This is my land, too. Decided to give it to him. Biggest mistake of my life, but that's my fault – I'm kind-hearted. Now if you wanted some land and a house built you'd only have to ask. "Beatty how about a house?" It's yours for the asking. What are you doing in town? Visiting?

MARY: Sort of.

BEATTY: Where are you living?

MARY: I'm at Brooks' at the moment.

BEATTY: Brooks' Hotel – that's my second home! Why haven't I seen you there?

MARY: I just arrived yesterday.

BEATTY: You and me should be at Brooks', not here. Or at my place – I'm just across the road. Maplewood – can't miss it. Sure you don't want a drink?

Mary shakes her head and steps back.

This is my house. I built it. My land.

20

Beatty approaches Mary.

If my brother-in-law's going to live in Brattle-boro, he'll have to learn a few things. Four years – he still hasn't learned. Give him time. British – they're slow learners. Like lobsters, which they are. You've got to put a peg in their claws.

MARY: He's your brother-in-law?

BEATTY: I can't help that. I went over to London when it was all happening – I told my sister he looked like a real crab-apple. In the end they made me go home. Beatty's making a ruckus, they said. They thought I was a right son-of-a-whore for trying to spoil things. As soon as he marched into this Christless house he's been a real Redcoat. And mean? Try to get a nickel out of him. I'm surprised he let you in. Of course, being here's going to cost you something. He'll charge you rent. How long have you been here? An hour or so? That'll be four dollars. Use of the chair? Another dollar. The firewood? Two bits. My brother-in-law's something special when it comes to money. My sister's worse. It's a different story when the booky people come, the Harvard people, the publishing people, Sherlock Holmes – he was here last year, Sherlock Holmes. I cooked him a turkey.

MARY: I take it you don't really get along too well.

BEATTY: Tolerably well. No buckshot yet. But President Cleveland's got the right idea. That man's going to make me a Democrat. At first I thought Cleveland was joking – just political hogwash.

MARY: Do you think Venezuela's worth fighting about?

BEATTY: They're dagoes, but never mind. Look at Cuba. There's going to be trouble there, too. It's not the places that matter – it's the Spanish, the English.

21

They used to run this country. They're treating the dagoes like they used to treat us. The Redcoat's treating me the same way. But this war will give us a chance to blow holy Jesus out of them. We've done it before and by God we'll do it again! You know where you are? This is the Green Mountains. This is where Ethan Allen and the Green Mountain Boys are from. When it happens again I'm going to be with them. It's going to end the same way – the lobsters boiled to a turn, with pegs in their claws. (*He walks towards Mary*) Want to help? You could be a big help.

MARY: Please – (*she fends Beatty off*)

BEATTY: (*with a leer*) Why don't you give us a hand?

MARY: (*backing up*) Mr. – Beatty, please.

BEATTY: (*attempts to kiss her*) What's wrong?

MARY: Please – not here.

BEATTY: (*touches her cheek*) How about right here?

MARY: I don't feel safe. (*Mary has now backed all the way to the door*)

BEATTY: Stay here. You're safe in Naulakha.

Mary looks worried.

She don't believe me. (*Firmly*) I don't want to kiss you, dearie.

Mary looks unconvinced.

She still don't believe me. I ain't peculiar. (*He eyes her*) She don't feel safe. All righty, then!

Beatty marches over to the fireplace and begins strapping on the skis.

Just to prove my intentions are pure – goddamn, I only want to talk to you! – I will tie these onto my clodhoppers – there! (*He stands up and then shuffles unsteadily a few paces*) Now do you feel safe?

MARY: That's better. (*She giggles at him*)

BEATTY: I sure as hell don't. (*He wobbles*) But I won't catch you on these things.

MARY: You look a sight! (*She reaches into her handbag, takes out a hanky and sneezes into it*)

BEATTY: *Gesundheit.* What business are you in?

MARY: I'm with the *Post.*

BEATTY: The Boston *Post?*

MARY: That's right. I'm a reporter.

BEATTY: A girl reporter? *Here?*

MARY: Yes, I –

Beatty begins to shake with laughter. He cannot speak he is laughing so hard.

– what's so funny? Why shouldn't a girl be a reporter? We've as much right to work for the papers as men. More right, really. Most of our readers are women, and that's the truth.

BEATTY: (*still laughing*) No, no –

MARY: I'm not new at it, either. I was in Boston for a year and then Worcester for almost ten months. That's why they moved me to Brattleboro. What have you got here. Just the *Phoenix* and its fat-stock shows and weddings and funerals and who's the new dog-catcher. The *Post*'s going to move in here and sell papers. I'll cover this part of Vermont and then people will have Vermont news *and* Boston news. You watch. There isn't going to be a *Phoenix* when we're through. It's not funny!

BEATTY: (*calming himself, but still giggling*) I'm not laughing at that.

23

MARY:	You think it's funny – a girl reporter? (*Beatty laughs*) There's lots of them around, if you'd care to leave this jerk-water town and open your eyes. All the papers have them.
BEATTY:	Not here.
MARY:	Brattleboro? I'm not surprised.
BEATTY:	Naulakha.
MARY:	I don't know what you mean.
BEATTY:	You didn't tell him, did you? The Redcoat. That you're a reporter.
MARY:	We were talking about more important things.
BEATTY:	Sure you were. You're a smart one, Mary. I give you credit for that. You got lost in the snow. He took you in. Lost in the snow! Just a case of sniffles –

Mary answers again.

	– but he's the one who's going to get frostbite. You didn't tell him.
MARY:	But I'm going to.
BEATTY:	What's the use? He'll love you all the same. You talk to him, and if there's anything you want to know I'll tell you. You doing an article?
MARY:	I'm not sure yet. But I had to see him. He's the most important man in town.
BEATTY:	Cowflap.
MARY:	I suppose *you* are.
BEATTY:	Some people think so. But no, I'm not. There hasn't been an important man in town since my grandfather died, six years ago. He was a great man, and rich – why, he'd put the Redcoat in the shade, let me tell you. He had a million dollars. When the Redcoat came here he didn't have a pot

to piss in. Anyway, since when are foreigners so important?

MARY: He's an important writer. Ask anyone.

BEATTY: I could write stories that would beat hell out of his. Runs in the family. My brother was a writer – better than the Redcoat by a country mile. Forget about him. But there are a lot of good people around – hayseeds, hogsloppers, I know them all. I think I can be some use to you. We can have some fun – why not?

No knock. Carrie enters just as Beatty is saying, "I can be some use". She speaks sharply.

CARRIE: Beatty!

BEATTY: Hello, sister. (*He stoops and unties the skis*)

CARRIE: What are you doing in here?

BEATTY: Mary and I were just chewing the fat.

CARRIE: (*to Mary*) Your dinner's ready, Miss Hackett. Just down the hall, in the dining room. You'd better hurry or it'll get cold.

MARY: Thank you so much. (*Mary leaves hurriedly*)

BEATTY: She's going to appreciate that. She seems a swell girl.

CARRIE: Do you know her?

BEATTY: If I say yes, you'll boot her out for fair! I never met her before in my life.

CARRIE: You have no business in here.

BEATTY: Does *she*? Come on, sister. If a stranger can come in here, surely a member of the family's welcome.

CARRIE: This room is private.

BEATTY: You don't know her from a hole in the ground.

CARRIE: Miss Hackett is a guest. It has nothing to do with you.

25

BEATTY: She's mighty pretty. What does the Redcoat think of her?

CARRIE: Mind that mouth of yours, Beatty. He's done a great deal for you.

BEATTY: Sure has. He let me give him ten acres. He let me build him a house. I'm grateful for that. And his sewer-pipe's draining sludge on my meadow. I really appreciate –

CARRIE: We paid for everything we got, including the land. As for the sewer-pipe – you laid it on your land, for fertilizer.

BEATTY: I don't want it anymore. I've got nothing to fertilize these days. Well, (*he snickers*) not a hell of a lot. Sister, you owe me forty dollars.

CARRIE: It's going to cost that to move the sewer-pipe; Rud told you to lay it so it emptied on our meadow. You didn't pay any attention to what he said. You wanted it and now you want it moved. So you can pay for it.

BEATTY: All the meadows are mine – this whole god-damned place is mine. You came here with no money at all, sister – and I helped you out. Now I want some help.

CARRIE: We've done nothing but help you out, give you money –

BEATTY: All you did was put me to work and charge me for it.

CARRIE: What work did you ever do?

BEATTY: You're living in it.

Kipling comes in breathlessly.

KIPLING: Carrie, there's a horse – (*sees Beatty, stiffens*) Hello, I see you've penetrated already. (*To Carrie*) Where is our friend?

26

CARRIE:	In the dining room.
KIPLING:	Good. Well, Beatty, how's the snow where you are?
BEATTY:	I don't know why you ask a question like that. You can spit to Maplewood from here – probably do. It's the same snow as yours.
CARRIE:	Have you got enough firewood?
BEATTY:	I'm down to my last cord.
KIPLING:	We'd be glad to help you out in that department. Matthew says we have more than enough.
BEATTY:	Don't you send that son-of-a-whore down to Maplewood.
CARRIE:	How is Mai, and little Marjorie?
KIPLING:	Yes, how is my darling Marjorie?
BEATTY:	Both of them whining to beat the band.
KIPLING:	What a dear child Marjorie is. I saw her in the snow yesterday, all bundled up in her coonskins –
BEATTY:	Look, can we talk about what's really on our minds instead of all this cowflap?
KIPLING:	(taken aback) I thought this was a social call.
BEATTY:	When I want to make social calls I don't generally come here. You owe me forty dollars.
KIPLING:	I find that hard to believe.
BEATTY:	Believe me, you do.
KIPLING:	(to Carrie) What does the Committee of Ways and Means say?
BEATTY:	(to Kipling) He doesn't even know!
CARRIE:	There is forty dollars outstanding. But he wants to move the sewer-pipe. I think that would just about settle the debt.

BEATTY: I don't give shit or shine about the sewer-pipe. I could plug it. That'd be fun for you. You owe me forty for work I've already done, and I demand payment, cash on the barrel-head.

KIPLING: (*to Carrie*) Let's pay and be done with it. I think we should clear the account. If the money is Beatty's, then he ought to have it.

BEATTY: Hearing that, anyone would take you for a straight-shooter. (*To Carrie*) Well, how about it, sister?

CARRIE: It's safe with us. It won't be safe with you. I know what you'd do with it.

BEATTY: It's no business of yours what I do with my money.

CARRIE: You'll buy liquor and treat your friends. You'll just scatter it, and Mai and little Marjorie won't see a red cent.

BEATTY: I'm trying to keep a roof over my head, don't you understand?

KIPLING: (*to Carrie*) Let's settle.

CARRIE: Forty dollars won't get him through the winter. No, paying him isn't the answer.

BEATTY: All right, don't pay me. (*Starts to leave*) I'm not going begging to you, or anyone. But you'll take the consequences. I'll plug that sewer-pipe so bad you'll be drowning. And then I'll be bankrupt and I'll yell it all over the state and I'll tell them why.

CARRIE: (*urging him back*) Beatty, come here.

KIPLING: Don't rush off.

BEATTY: I've got nothing more to say.

CARRIE: *I* do, sonny.

BEATTY: You didn't even offer me a drink. That's all I'm worth.

KIPLING: (*pouring a drink*) Here, have some sherry. It's good British stuff, from the best wine merchant in St. James's. (*Sees his error*) Well, it's a jolly sight better than cider.

BEATTY: (*taking the glass*) Thanks. (*Drinks it at a gulp*) What is it, then?

CARRIE: Rud and I know you've been through a trying time. You say we're ungrateful, but you're wrong. We haven't forgotten that you were the first person we met here.

BEATTY: I met your train. It was thirty below. Where were the rest of them that night? You would have froze.

KIPLING: I'll never forget that – you on your sleigh. Those coonskin coats and earflaps, and that woolpack we sat on. There was nothing but snow under the moon.

BEATTY: You looked like you were pole-axed!

KIPLING: I'd never seen anything like it. I thought, this is the only place I want to live.

CARRIE: (*to Beatty*) We couldn't have built this house without you.

BEATTY: Damn right. Wouldn't have had the land, either. Or the wood, or the labor. Or me picking up your mail or putting down your sewer-pipe.

CARRIE: We've tried to do our best for you. I hope you realize that.

BEATTY: (*to Kipling*) I've heard it both ways.

CARRIE: We're grateful to you for helping us settle here. This is our first home and it means an awful lot to us. You've been splendid, Beatty.

BEATTY: (*to Kipling*) It's interesting to hear you say that, sister, because I've heard it different. It's one thing up in Naulakha. It's another thing in town.

29

But maybe both of you don't see eye to eye where I'm concerned.

KIPLING: Please do listen. I'm in agreement with Carrie, a hundred percent.

CARRIE: You've got your faults, Beatty. You have to admit that.

BEATTY: Maybe I talk too much, but at least I don't do it out of the side of my mouth.

KIPLING: This is getting us nowhere.

CARRIE: We won't rake over the past. All I'm saying is that you've given us help when we needed it. And now we're settled, and, frankly, we're in a position to help you.

BEATTY: It's just forty bucks in the collection-plate. I could do without the preaching.

CARRIE: Even if you spend it wisely, which I doubt, it'll be gone by January and you'll be around here again looking for more – as sure as shooting. You won't have enough for feed, you'll be done to selling your horses and then you'll have nothing to plow with. A farmer without credit is as lame as an old mule and you know it. You can't raise money on corn shucks and windfall apples.

BEATTY: I'll make cider with windfalls and smoke the shucks in my pipe.

KIPLING: We're prepared to help you, but first you've got to help yourself.

BEATTY: That's what I've been doing all along, haven't I?

CARRIE: Without much noticeable effect. You've got to try a bit harder. Beatty, we're willing to advance you a certain sum if you change your ways.

BEATTY: I'm asking for a certain sum. You heard the gentleman here – it's mine by rights.

CARRIE: We're not talking about forty dollars anymore.

30

BEATTY: (*to Kipling*) How much are you talking about?

KIPLING: (*confounded by the question*) Carrie?

CARRIE: Ten thousand dollars.

BEATTY: Now you're talking! (*Excited*) Now you're talk-
           ing! That's more like it. Shoot! (*Suspiciously*)
           What do I have to do in return? There's always a
           catch with you.

CARRIE: Dry up, for one thing.

BEATTY: (*still grinning*) I'll do my best. Seems worth it for
           ten grand. Anything's worth that.

CARRIE: There'll be no half measures. No hard liquor –
           that's the first thing. I think if you stop your
           drinking you'll stop your swearing.

BEATTY: If I stop my drinking I'll be swearing like a
           goddamned trooper and won't have the strength
           to pull a greasy string out of a duck's ass. But I
           can try. Show me that money and I'll be a perfect
           angel.

CARRIE: And you've got to find yourself a decent job. I
           mean something proper, maybe real estate.

BEATTY: Why I was thinking about that very thing
           yesterday afternoon! I was talking to George
           Hitt. He said to me, "Balestier, how come you
           never took up the law? You sure have a way with
           words." I said, "George, I'm thinking of going
           into real estate – that's what Brattleboro needs.
           As soon as the trams are running, people are
           going to be flocking to this town."

KIPLING: If the trams come, I go.

BEATTY: Then you'll have something to go on.

CARRIE: If you're going to get a fresh start you'll have to
           find a new town. A clean slate, away from your
           cronies and those spongers.

31

BEATTY: I've got to leave Brattleboro? Is that what you're asking?

CARRIE: Beatty, it's for your own good. You weren't born here – your roots aren't very deep. You could go back to Rochester, or somewhere in New York. If you don't want to go far you could try Worcester, or Burlington. They're growing, and you could grow with them. Use the ten thousand to set yourself up in business.

BEATTY: Buy at ten, sell at twenty. It might work. Sometimes I miss Rochester. Then I remember Mother's still there and I stop missing it. There's some good horse country in Massachusetts, but Massachusetts people talk so much cowflap. If I agree to your conditions I get the money, is that it?

CARRIE: Ten thousand dollars is more than we have –

BEATTY: (*exploding*) What the Jesus are we talking about then!

CARRIE: Let me finish. But we can raise it. If you go to the bank and ask for ten thousand they'll laugh. Even if you use your farm as collateral the most you'll get is three – four at the outside. Which is a shame, because Maplewood is worth six thousand, furnished and free of mortgage.

BEATTY: I could get seven.

CARRIE: We're offering you ten.

BEATTY: You're buying my farm?

CARRIE: We're proposing to. We're willing to pay much more than the market price.

BEATTY: I won't have any place to live.

CARRIE: You'll have capital and you'll be sober. You've got a good head. In a new town you could blaze trails.

32

BEATTY: Money talks.

KIPLING: Consider it a dowry. Irish, Germans, Italians have come to this country with much less than that – with nothing but an unintelligible accent. They've managed. All it takes is work. Before long, you'll be on your own feet and you can think about other things.

BEATTY: I could write my stories. Wolcott always said I had talent. *I* could be a writer.

KIPLING: With a little application, a little capital. It's possible. You might have the demon.

CARRIE: He's got the demon.

BEATTY: All this sounds fine, but I've got a wife and child. (*To Kipling*) When you came here you didn't have a child. It's a complication. I'm not a gypsy – I can't just fold my tent and light out. I've got to think of Marjorie.

CARRIE: We've considered that. It's our last proposal. We understand the difficulty of starting afresh. Your wife will be a great help to you. But Marjorie might be a burden. Children aren't very portable creatures, Beatty. We're prepared to keep Marjorie. She and Josephine get along fine – and soon we'll have another. We're got plenty of room, and nannies and – why this is Marjorie's second home. She'd love it here.

BEATTY: (*to Kipling*) Whose idea was this?

KIPLING: The Committee of Ways and Means.

BEATTY: Both of you?

CARRIE: It's the best way to handle it, Beatty. Trust in us.

BEATTY: I'll have to talk it over with Mai. She might not like it.

KIPLING: You can convince her.

BEATTY: (*pointedly*) She might have a good reason for not liking it.

KIPLING: Let's drop the subject for the moment, shall we?

BEATTY: Fine with me. My head hurts. But I've given you a hearing. Now listen – I'm flat broke. If I don't have five dollars, you're going to hear screams from Maplewood.

CARRIE: (*taking out her purse*) This is positively the last time.

BEATTY: Make it ten. Then you'll only owe me thirty.

Mary Hackett enters.

MARY: Excuse me.

KIPLING: Come in. This is Mr. Balestier.

BEATTY: I've had the pleasure already.

MARY: Yes, we –

KIPLING: Do tell.

BEATTY: A little while ago, I came looking for you –

CARRIE: (*to Kipling*) I was in the kitchen.

BEATTY: I found Mary in here. She was just curled up in front of the fireplace, unfreezing her bones.

KIPLING: We're glad to have her aboard.

MARY: Your cook served me a delicious meal. She's not an American either – is she Scotch, too? Gosh, it's a whole houseful of foreigners! (*Thinks again*) I guess I'm the only foreigner.

BEATTY: (*breaking the silence*) You and me. Oh, they'll look after you at Brooks'.

CARRIE: You're at the hotel?

MARY: It was recommended.

CARRIE: I thought, as it's nearly Christmas, you might be staying with relatives.

MARY: I don't have any relatives in Brattleboro. I don't know a soul, except you and Mr. Kipling. And Beatty. I consider myself real lucky. As long as there's a church in town I'll be all right for Christmas.

KIPLING: The church is Unitarian.

MARY: Then I'll find a rock and pray behind it.

BEATTY: That's Unitarianism.

CARRIE: (to Beatty) They'll be expecting you at Maplewood – wondering what happened to you.

BEATTY: They know where I am.

CARRIE: (to Mary) It's getting rather late. And it's a long way back to town.

KIPLING: We might be able to make room.

MARY: I've been enough trouble already.

KIPLING: It's no bother. And we didn't finish our little chat, did we?

MARY: (to Carrie) Mr. Kipling thinks there's going to be a war.

BEATTY: The Redcoats are coming! (To Mary) We're related to Paul Revere – her and me. He (indicates Kipling) was on the other side. Yep, that's the enemy there, puffing his pipe.

KIPLING: I wouldn't have thought this was a joking matter. And you might be surprised at the outcome.

BEATTY: Depends. The Redcoats might have already planted spies. That'll be a problem – British spies, reporting on our defenses. Sending back information. Must be a lot of Benedict Arnolds around Brattleboro, pretending to be friendly and writing coded messages and –

CARRIE: Shut it, Beatty.

KIPLING: (to Mary) Beatty's got quite a lively imagination.

BEATTY: (*to Mary*) Oh, I wasn't referring to Mr. Kipling. Of course, he does have some important friends in Washington. He's powerfully interested in the U.S. Army, and he keeps his ear to the ground. But, no, m'am, he never pretended to be friendly.

MARY: (*uneasy*) Did I leave my bag somewhere in here? That snow gave me a terrible case of sneezes.

BEATTY: I thought I saw it over there by the fire.

KIPLING: (*moving to the chair where Mary was sitting*) Here it is. It's a proper saddlebag.

MARY: It's got all my things.

KIPLING: (*picking up the notebook from his desk*) Is this yours?

MARY: (*taking the bag and notebook*) Yes, thank you.

KIPLING: I recognize that notebook. I used to have one like that. That's a short-hand notebook.

MARY: Yes, sir.

KIPLING: You know short-hand, do you?

MARY: Oh yes. I learned it in Boston. At Katie Gibbs.

KIPLING: (*with deep suspicion*) I had a notebook like that in India. Lahore. Needed it for my job. Miss Hackett, you're not a secretary, are you?

MARY: No, sir, I'm not.

KIPLING: Then you must be from the *Sewer*.

CARRIE: Rud –

MARY: Pardon?

KIPLING: I said, the *Sewer*.

BEATTY: Oh, boy –

CARRIE: Rud, please. (*To Mary*) You'd better go.

KIPLING: Or is it the *Stabber*, or the *Family Spy*, or the *New York Private Listener* –

36

MARY: I don't know what you –

KIPLING: Or the *New York Peeper*, or the *Plunderer*, the *Keyhole Reporter*, the *Rowdy Journal*?

MARY: I'm from the *Post*.

KIPLING: They sent you up here, did they?

MARY: They didn't send me. I wanted –

KIPLING: All the way from New York!

MARY: I'm not from – !

KIPLING: (*eyeing Mary closely, then walking around her*) Here's the New York papers! Here's full particulars of the patriotic loco-foco movement yesterday, in which the Whigs was so chawed up. And the Alabama gouging case. And the interesting Arkansas dooel, with Bowie knives. Here she is. Here's the papers. Here's the *Sewer*'s exposure of the Washington Gang, and the *Sewer*'s account of a flagrant act of dishonesty committed by the Secretary of State when he was eight years old – now communicated at great expense, by his own nurse! Here's the *Sewer* with a whole column of New Yorkers to be shown up, and all their names printed! Here's the *Sewer*'s article upon the judge that tried him, day afore yesterday, for libel, and the *Sewer*'s tribute to the independent account of what might have been expected if they had! Here's the wide-awake *Sewer*, always on the look-out, the leading journal of the United States. (*To Carrie*) Here she is – here's the New York papers!

MARY: I'm from Boston.

KIPLING: What did you say your name was? Scudder? Pogram? Brick?

MARY: Mary Hackett, sir.

KIPLING: Dickens couldn't have named you better than that.

CARRIE:	(*to Kipling*) Rud – please!
KIPLING:	Out you go, young lady.
BEATTY:	It's still snowing!
KIPLING:	Call Matthew –
MARY:	Mr. Kipling, please give me a chance. I came up here for no other reason than to see you.
KIPLING:	You said you were lost.
MARY:	I *got* lost.
KIPLING:	You're wasting my time.
MARY:	I was hoping you'd let me interview you.
KIPLING:	You said nothing about that. You were speaking about the weather. Taking a professional interest in the contents of my house and my head.
MARY:	I am genuinely interested in your poems.
KIPLING:	Then use the public library.
MARY:	Please –
KIPLING:	I decline to be interviewed. It is an outrage to be insulted in one's own home and asked to give the details of one's private life. Haven't you people cheated me enough? Your copyright laws have swindled me out of considerable money. Is it not enough to steal my books without intruding on my private life?
MARY:	I'm sorry for the intrusion. I wanted to write something.
KIPLING:	I have not entirely abandoned the habit of saying what I want to say under my own signature.
MARY:	(*preparing to go*) I enjoyed talking with you, Mr. –
KIPLING:	It's not for sale. Don't you publish it, or you'll find yourself and the *Sewer* in court! I don't talk

38

to strangers. When I have anything to say, I write it down and sell it. My brains are my own!

Mary is stunned into silence.

Take her out of here.

BEATTY: I was just leaving. (*to Mary*) I'll show you the way.

Mary and Beatty leave.

CARRIE: (*with disapproval*) Rud – why?

KIPLING: There will be a war, don't you know. And she's going to start it. And if she doesn't, your beloved brother will.

Scene 2

The distant sound of a railway train. The whistle, twice. The study again, about noon, three days later: Christmas Day. Matthew enters, carrying a tray of clean glasses. He goes to the drinks cupboard, sets out the glasses, and then checks the decanters. He moves to the mantelpiece, which is festive with Christmas decorations, scrutinizes the statue of the wolf, then moves it as if trying to conceal it behind a sprig of holly. The wolf retains its look of lupine menace. Matthew removes a ribbon from the shaft of a candle and ties it in a gay bow around the wolf's neck.

As he knots the bow, Kipling enters. He wears black patent-leather shoes, striped formal trousers and a stiff shirt. He carries his evening jacket over his arm, and proffers his black tie.

KIPLING: I wonder if you would mind terribly doing that for me.

HOWARD: Pardon, sir?

KIPLING: A bow, Matthew. (*Indicates the beribboned wolf*) Like that.

HOWARD: Right you are, sir.

   In most of the dialogue that follows, Matthew stands over Kipling, tying his tie, picking pieces of lint from Kipling's trousers, brushing the jacket, and generally fussing. He is acting the part of a servant, but much of what he says is instructive and cautioning to Kipling.

40

KIPLING: They hate us, Matthew, these Americans.

HOWARD: I fancy they do, sir.

KIPLING: With their whole soul.

HOWARD: Mustn't complain, sir.

KIPLING: I didn't come to this country with the intention of enduring that. Have you ever thought what will happen if there's a war?

HOWARD: I expect there will be a war, sir. People in town are mentioning it.

KIPLING: That puts us in a delightful position, doesn't it?

HOWARD: They know how to talk, sir. But I don't reckon they can do much else.

KIPLING: They're armed! Every fool in Brattleboro owns a shotgun. And they're fighting mad. I've seen them maniacal on cider.

HOWARD: I take no notice of them. (*Helps Kipling into his jacket*)

KIPLING: (*justifying himself*) I don't preoccupy myself with them. But the guns —

HOWARD: (*still brushing lint away*) I've been in grouse-moors where every gentleman had a gun, sir. Up at dawn. I supervised the hampers. All day I'd hear the shouts, the dogs, the ghillies cursing, the blooming lot. But some days, driving back, there wasn't a single bird in the pouch. It was queer. Even a gentleman with a shotgun can be made to look a fool.

KIPLING: Still, the season was on. The grouse can't have felt very cheerful. I pray to God it won't come to that. But I must confess I do think about it. Did you hear the train whistle?

HOWARD: Yes, sir, the New York train.

KIPLING: That's the down-train. The up-train's to Canada.

41

HOWARD: Canada, sir?

KIPLING: A British subject might be better off in British territory.

HOWARD: With all respect, sir. If there's a war, Canada will fight. She'll show the flag, sir.

KIPLING: And we'll be in the line of fire.

HOWARD: (*straightens Kipling's tie*) I won't bolt, sir.

KIPLING: Of course not. Nor will I. But it does make one think.

HOWARD: I reckon I'll stay right here with you, sir, on the same basis.

KIPLING: (*still uneasy*) Yes, yes.

HOWARD: It's a good house, is Naulakha. I can't see abandoning the old girl to them. I think the people here are capable of doing her a damage if we left her untended. Your horses, your books, your property, sir.

KIPLING: (*bitterly*) So we go to ground. (*With resolve*) But white men don't go to ground!

HOWARD: No, sir. Was there anything else, sir?

KIPLING: (*taking an envelope out of his pocket*) We're spending Boxing Day down the road. So I'll give you your *baksheesh* now.

HOWARD: Thank you, sir. God bless, and a Happy Christmas to you.

KIPLING: Has Mrs. Balestier been seen to?

HOWARD: Yes, sir. Plenty of room for her. I wish I could say the same for the horses. What with Doctor Conland's team, I don't think we could squeeze in one more animal.

KIPLING: We'll use the Beechwood stables if we find we're stretched.

HOWARD: I was thinking of Mr. Beatty's team, sir.

KIPLING: I'll worry about Beatty. You give him a wide berth. He'll only be rude to you.

HOWARD: Makes no odds, sir.

A knock.

KIPLING: Enter!

Dr. Conland enters carrying a medical man's satchel and a stethoscope of the period. The doctor is in his fifties, white-haired but very hardy. He could be a ship's captain.

Doctor Conland, Matthew here was just saying your team of horses like Naulakha's stable fare so well they're singing.

CONLAND: Very kind of you, Matthew. Merry Christmas.

HOWARD: And to you, sir. (*He leaves*)

KIPLING: What's the verdict, James?

CONLAND: If the heartbeat is any indicator, you're going to have yourself a real bouncer in a fortnight or so. Carrie seems to be fine.

KIPLING: She has her hands full with that brother of hers. James, I appreciate your looking after Carrie. You know, I didn't invite you over here on false pretenses – this is Christmas. Yours isn't supposed to be a professional visit.

CONLAND: I'm glad to oblige. I'm only sorry your Christmas got off to such a bad start.

KIPLING: Was I raving last night? I expect I was.

CONLAND: (*laughing*) You said, "In this country, there is no liberty and no equality – only fraternity."

KIPLING: Don't hold it against me. I like this country. As the nigger said in Court, "If I didn't like de woman, how come I take de trouble to hit her on de haid." James, take a pew.

43

Conland sits.

And a drop of amontillado. (*Kipling pours drinks*) The ladies will be here by and by. (*Hands Conland the drink*)

CONLAND: Season's greetings. She was Irish, you say?

KIPLING: Yes, that should have been sufficient warning. Carrie was on her guard from the outset, I couldn't believe that the Irish had taken it up. I thought they'd gone straight from saloon-keeping to politics. That seemed to suit their instincts of secrecy, plunder and anonymous denunciation.

CONLAND: Don't be too hard on them. We're a whole country of immigrants.

KIPLING: You're no immigrant, James. You're a white man.

CONLAND: We all come by the same route, Westward-bound on ship-board.

KIPLING: Your ships were not their ships.

CONLAND: The very same.

KIPLING: Dishwater! Your ancestors came under sail. They were sifted and salted by the long voyage – a month or more. Why don't Americans see this? That was a real education, sailing across the Atlantic. It wasn't kind, but it gave you some strong men. When the sails came down and steam began – in the early Seventies – then the band began to play. Steaming across the Atlantic the same as sail? No, James – then the passengers turned into human cargo, like tea-chests or so many coils of jute, from every bog in Ireland and every ghetto ant-hill. Now they're delivered with all their imperfections, with all their infections, in a fortnight. Those are the people who want war.

44

CONLAND: This war fever will blow over. We've been through it before. You give us a few years and you'll see. We can ride out this storm.

KIPLING: Cleveland means to have a war. He and his Secretary of State are cooking it up together. If you can't start a love affair, start a row, eh?

CONLAND: You're deceiving yourself. And the people here look up to you.

KIPLING: Oh, we're excellent friends, me and the aborigines. But they can't understand why I don't come to chicken suppers and church sociables and turkey sprees.

CONLAND: That doesn't count for much.

KIPLING: I believe they hold it against me.

CONLAND: If that was so, I'd know it, and I've heard no such thing.

KIPLING: You haven't been talking to Beatty.

CONLAND: (*dismissively*) Oh, Beatty.

KIPLING: No one loves this town more than I do, but – it seems to me – there's an immense and unacknowledged boredom at the back of it all, the dead weight of material things passionately worked up into gods. Beatty hates me.

CONLAND: He's got quite a few friends in town.

KIPLING: He means to make war on me.

CONLAND: Very popular with the cracker-barrel set. Yes, they consider that boy a regular riot. And not only the hayseeds.

KIPLING: They forgive him his noise, Why don't they forgive me my silence. I don't *like* turkey sprees!

CONLAND: Brattleboro's always been partial to jokesters.

As Conland speaks, Beatty appears at stage-left. Conland cannot see him, but Kipling can. Beatty

45

is speaking apparently to a group of people, whom we can't see.

BEATTY: So he sticks the pipe up the ass of the cross-eyed mule and blows and blows. Then he goes up front, but the eyes are still crossed. "Maybe you ain't blowing hard enough," says the farmer, and goes back, takes the pipe out of the mule's ass and turns it around and sticks it back in and starts blowing. "Wait a minute," says the hayseed. "Why did you turn that pipe around? Why the Jesus are you blowing on *that* end?" The farmer looks at him. He says, "I don't want to get your germs – you had your mouth on the other end."

CONLAND: Beatty makes them laugh.

KIPLING: (*regarding Beatty, who turns and comes closer*) Bullies are always failed comedians. I know them. They were virtually the first people I met in England. I was – what? Six or seven. I couldn't see straight. I didn't have these gig-lamps then. I was living with a pair of brutes in Southsea – mother and son. He was the spit of Beatty.

Looks closely at Beatty, who smirks.

A cynically immoral hog. His conduct was blatant indecency.

She'd finish with me, then he'd roast me on the other side. I was a natural victim – I was alone, away from home, in a strange place. He hung a sign on my back. *Liar*, it said. He made me wear it through the streets of Southsea.

Beatty puts his foot crudely on the arm of a chair and sets his face at Kipling.

BEATTY: Why don't you go home, Redcoat? You don't belong. You're a nearsighted midget. You married my sister for her money – she doesn't have anything else. She's got a face like the back of

46

a barn. You're just making a fool of yourself. Why don't you go home?

Kipling turns away from Beatty.

KIPLING: I knew what terror was. No boy can stand the torture of one unvarying question – that's the essence of bullying. It's Cleveland's technique, you notice. I'd never been so frightened. I was so far away. I blubbed –

Beatty is laughing silently, as Kipling glances at him.

CONLAND: A lot of so-called bullying is just thoughtlessness –

KIPLING: No! Bullies love bullying! There's thought in it – don't talk like a padre. (*Mockingly*) "They never really bully –" No, only knock 'em about a little bit. Only kick their souls out of them, and they go and blub in the boxrooms. Shove their heads into their ulsters and blub. Write home three times a day, begging to be taken away. *I've* done that. I was at school.

BEATTY: I'll bet you were a goddamned little horror, too.

CONLAND: But Beatty's generous –

KIPLING: (*to Beatty*) The bleating of the kid excites the tiger.

CONLAND: – he'd give you the shirt off his back.

KIPLING: (*to Beatty*) I learned a thing or two, then. I learned to educate bullies. And I was never afraid again. (*To Conland*) It's not his shirt. That's not generosity – it's theft. He used to be artful about his cadging, but now –

BEATTY: You owe me money. Cough it up, or I'll make you sing –

KIPLING: I won't give him any more.

BEATTY: Why don't you just go home!

KIPLING: It's very worrying for Carrie. And in her condition!

BEATTY: Home – over there! (*Beatty is backing away*)

KIPLING: But we took a cue from Lord Salisbury. We're not giving in. We've offered the boy terms.

CONLAND: Has he accepted?

Kipling looks at Beatty. Beatty shrugs and leaves.

KIPLING: He'll have to. It's more than we should have done. A fellow like Beatty doesn't deserve second chances. (*Pause*) I've been carrying him for over three years.

Just as Beatty has vanished, Conland rises from the chair and sees Kipling staring in the direction Beatty has gone.

CONLAND: You're taking this Beatty business all too seriously. You've got a wonderful house – you're settled here. You've made something of this place, Rudyard.

KIPLING: Burdened myself with it.

CONLAND: I know you get pestered by the papers, but that's part of being famous. And look at you – thirty-one years old. When I was thirty-one I was up to here in fish-scales – gutting fish off the Grand Banks –

KIPLING: It's not just a question of robbery. I do believe he wants to destroy me. Isn't that the bully's ambition?

CONLAND: It's idleness. (*Pointedly*) Don't make the great mistake of listening to his jawing.

KIPLING: If a man sets out to destroy you, he won't necessarily succeed. But he can do a lot of damage. Even if he's not a white man.

CONLAND: That boy's idea of recreation is to go down to Flat Street and spend the afternoon spitting on

48

the sidewalk. He'll never grow up. He may have some bad in him, but he'll always be innocent – he's too weak to be guilty. I'm surprised at you, Rudyard, I really am. If you don't cooperate, there is no way he can hurt you.

KIPLING: (*with feeling*) No. But the damn fool doesn't seem to realize that I can hurt him!

CONLAND: My guess is that he's hurt already –

KIPLING: The bleating of the kid excites the tiger. I was at school. I got it worse than anyone. If you want an authority on bullying, come to me. Corkscrews, brush-drill, keys, head-knuckling, arm-twisting, rocking, ag-ags – and all the rest of it. But I learned. Want to know what education is? It's bullying the bully. There were two at school, Sefton and Campbell. The padre asked us to use our influence. We used our knuckles. Found one buzzing books at his fag and making him sing, another was gloriously applying the arm-twist to a piteous kid. We tricked them into a cock-fight, and when they were well and truly trussed up we turned on them, my comrades and I. They thought they knew about bullying. We taught them about bullying! First the corkscrews – no corkscrew is used. Then brush-drill – no brush is used – the torture is excessive. Then knuckles and rocking. We had them on the floor, and beat their hind ends with stumps. How they squealed! I drew blood from Campbell, and Sefton – we took off his mustache – burnt it. We watched them writhe in agony. I mean writhe, I mean agony. They had never been bullied, but now they were being treated to it. They'd never blubbed – but they were blubbing now, by gum. (*Kipling has become excited, telling this. He pauses.*) Then, while they were still blubbing, we dropped into chairs and watched them . . . luxuriously. If the chaplain had used that – moral suasion – he'd have been clapped in Bideford jail. But of course we got away with it. It wasn't a matter for the chaplain. We'd educated them boy to boy. And do you know – the bullying ceased. (*Pause*) I'll educate him.

CONLAND: You could make it worse. I don't want to see that.

KIPLING: He's as lawless as . . . your president.

CONLAND: (*soothingly*) You ever lived in the country before this?

KIPLING: No, only civilized places – Bombay, Allahabad, Lahore. This is the only home I've ever owned!

CONLAND: You've got cabin fever. It's the snow and the indoors.

KIPLING: I like the snow. It keeps the aborigines away. You needn't look at me like that. I'm quite sane.

CONLAND: You want to get out a bit. Oh, it's quite natural to feel the way you do – you're suffering Carrie's confinement. I'm going to take you on a trip. That's what you need.

KIPLING: (*desperately*) Listen, I'm between two barrels, like a pheasant. If the American barrel goes off it means dirt and slush and an untimely death across the Canada border. It's not cabin fever I've got – it's battle fatigue. And I look down (*looks at his desk*) and see that I am armed with nothing more efficient than a notebook, a stylo-graphic pen, and a pair of opera glasses. (*Pause*) I used to think I had a good wholesome life here. (*Suddenly*) I won't leave! I won't bolt! Why should I? I made this house.

CONLAND: I know the cure for you.

KIPLING: It ain't in that satchel, Doctor.

CONLAND: Right you are. It's in Gloucester. I like being a saw-bones, but the first work I ever did was the best. My uncle owned a cod-schooner out of Gloucester, the *Pocahontas*. He invited me on a run out to the Grand Banks. I was little more than a passenger then, and I was mighty sick – I fed the fishes! But on the next trip I learned to cut the cod and prepare them for the hold, and I wasn't sick at all. I was at it for eight years, on and off. Even after I started medical school I used to go out fishing. For my nerves.

KIPLING: On the schooner?

CONLAND: Anything going. Sometimes on a pollock-fisher, which is an experience. They're real scows. I got to know the sea around the Banks as well as I knew the country around Monadnock. I still have the charts.

KIPLING: We could go down together.

CONLAND: I'd love to. There might be a book in it for you.

KIPLING: I don't need another book, but this would be something to look forward to. We couldn't go before the birth.

CONLAND: The boats are iced-up now in any case. No, we'll have plenty of time to study the charts.

KIPLING: James, that'll be larks.

CONLAND: Gloucester's the prettiest little seaport you've ever seen. It's a picture, it really is.

KIPLING: To the New Year. (*He toasts with his glass*) To Gloucester!

CONLAND: It'll be a good year. You're going to be a father again.

Carrie and Mrs. Balestier enter. Mrs. Balestier, Carrie's mother, is a dignified woman in her sixties; a widow, wearing black.

KIPLING: (*self-conscious with his glass*) Purely medicinal, as the doctor here will testify. (*Embraces Mrs.*

51

Balestier) Welcome to Naulakha, Mother. Good trip?

MRS.
BALESTIER: Snow all the way from Rochester.

KIPLING: You'll be warm here. Carrie's got all the fires going.

CARRIE: Doctor Conland, I'm sure you remember my mother.

CONLAND: I surely do. How are you, Mrs. Balestier?

MRS.
BALESTIER: Frozen to my marrow, Doctor. I'll be glad to see the spring.

CONLAND: Won't we all!

KIPLING: Winter's only four days old. Spring will be a long time coming.

MRS.
BALESTIER: (*to Kipling*) Carrie's told me all your news. Isn't she looking well. I'm going to be a grandmother again! But I don't feel a bit old – not a bit. It really does give me a lift to see you all. And isn't Josephine getting to be a little lady.

KIPLING: Where is my angel?

CARRIE: She's eating, Rud. She said she was hungry. I thought it best if she went ahead and ate.

KIPLING: As long as she leaves some for us. She's got quite an appetite.

CONLAND: She's blooming, all right. I looked over her this morning. I must admit I was anxious to hear her talk – what's going to come out, English or American? I said, "What with all this snow, I bet you miss playing in the grass." She says, "We call it grahss."

KIPLING: I do, but no one else does! No, she's a half-breed, there's no denying that. Now what will you ladies drink? I can offer amontillado, fino, or a rather dubious sweet one I picked up in New York.

MRS.
BALESTIER: I won't have a drink just now, Rudyard, thank you.

KIPLING: Carrie? (*to Conland*) That is, Doctor, if you have no objection.

CONLAND: No one pays attention to doctors at Christmas.

CARRIE: I've just had some fruit juice. (*To Mrs. B.*) It was the same when I was carrying Josephine. I had a passion for fruit juice.

KIPLING: It's a throw-back, don't you know. My children have the tropics in their veins. How is that unborn infant to know it's not in Bombay? Well, it won't be long. And then James and I are going to have a look at Gloucester. He's been spinning me yarns of his days on the cod-schooners. He doesn't recommend pollock-fishers at all.

MRS.
BALESTIER: If you're interested in fishing you should hop over to Lake Winnipesaukee. My late husband used to get some wonderful fishing there.

CONLAND: The idea is to leave the mainland. Salt air and the green waters of the Grand Banks. That's the prescription.

MRS.
BALESTIER: Good luck to you. I always thank my stars I have you living here. I don't think I could face another Atlantic crossing.

CONLAND: Rudyard was just telling me how easy it was for people to get from Europe to America. "Delivered with all their imperfections in a fortnight" – his very words.

KIPLING: I was speaking of the easefulness of steerage, not the rigors of first-class.

They laugh; Mrs. Balestier approaches Kipling.

MRS.
BALESTIER: Carrie was telling me you'd had a visitor.

KIPLING: Yes, I seem to be a magnet for every amateur pirate in the neighborhood. But what could I do? I had no idea I was being plundered. I'm a cork in the water! Oh, I lost my temper. I should have lost it sooner and used my boot on her backside –

CARRIE: Mother means Beatty.

KIPLING: I do apologize. I thought you were referring to – yes, Beatty was here. He's hale and hearty. Wish I could say the same for his bank balance.

MRS.
BALESTIER: Beatty doesn't change. He is nothing like Wolcott. At Beatty's age, Wolcott was running a publishing firm in London and meeting the best people. But Beatty was always the way he is now. I thought when he got married and moved out of Rochester he'd make something of himself.

KIPLING: Being a householder made a man of me. Why, Carrie and me –

MRS.
BALESTIER: People aren't the same. And it's wrong to want people to be different from what they are.

CARRIE: Beatty's still young. He'll settle down.

KIPLING: Or someone will settle him down.

MRS.
BALESTIER: Beatty's his own worst enemy. No one knows that better than I do.

CARRIE: Doctor Conland, you must forgive us for talking this way.

CONLAND: Please, I don't wish –

MRS.
BALESTIER: Oh, Doctor Conland's part of the family. Anyway, it's impossible to shock a medical man. He's heard me moan like this before – the same subject.

KIPLING: There is no other subject around here.

CONLAND: Do go on. I do promise not to take sides. I'll just stand by and treat the wounded.

MRS.
BALESTIER: I trust there won't be any casualties. Rudyard, I'm going to be as frank with you as I have been with Carrie. I came to bring some sort of reconciliation to this neck of the woods. I don't like the stories I've been hearing. I know they don't originate with you, but that doesn't matter. Even before Wolcott died there was a strain between Carrie and Beatty, and your moving here hasn't improved things. This isn't news to you, Doctor Conland. I doubt whether it's news to anyone between here and Chicago. I know he doesn't deserve it, but I want to give Beatty a chance – not for his sake, but for mine. A family jar is a terrible thing.

KIPLING: I daresay. I'm not used to bickering. Maybe that's why I'm so bad at it.

MRS.
BALESTIER: You've been wonderful. It's for Carrie to decide whether there'll be peace in the family.

CARRIE: I would have thought Beatty had something to do with it. And there's Mai – she's not the easiest person to deal with. Why, she hasn't been over here for months. I was surprised when she accepted this invitation for Christmas – I almost thought she'd refuse. She's done just about everything she can to make life –

KIPLING: Now, Carrie –

55

MRS.
BALESTIER: Let's start the New Year right. (*To Kipling*)
Carrie said that you'd made Beatty a proposition.
That's what the boy needs. I only wish I had it in
me to put things right. You're a generous and
thoughtful man, Rudyard, as all the world
knows. I'm counting on you to be patient with
my son and daughter, and help them bury the
hatchet. That's what Wolcott would have done.
You're like him in so many ways. (*Looks at the
skis*) What *are* those things?

KIPLING: They are a European invention that I predict will
revolutionize American winters. Skis. That's not
the whole apparatus. You need poles and gloves.

CARRIE: You also need a very hard bottom.

CONLAND: Rudyard promised me a turn, but it seems the
snow has to be a certain texture – not too hard or
too soft.

KIPLING: That was an excuse. I've only got one pair. I have
a feeling, if I let you try them, they'd end up as
kindling wood and we'd be looking for a new
doctor. (*To Mrs. B.*) You can fly like the wind on
these. We used them last week on Wantastiquet.
I've still got the bruises! Yes, (*points out the
window*) we were right over on that slope,
thundering along. Carrie's not in a fit state to use
them, so she was content to watch me humiliate
myself – say, that's Beatty on the porch.

MRS.
BALESTIER: He never was one to be punctual.

Beatty shouts from a distant room.

BEATTY'S
VOICE: Where the hell are you!

MRS.
BALESTIER: Or to stand on ceremony.

CARRIE: (*calling through the door*) In here! The library!

56

Beatty enters, still wearing his scarf. He is in his usual clothes, in contrast to the formality of the others. He wears boots, an old jacket, no tie; he carries a pumpkin.

BEATTY: There's usually a flunky down there waiting to make a face at me. Where are they today, sister? Hello, Mother. (*Kisses her, gives her the pumpkin*) This is for you. Merry Christmas. This jack-o'-lantern ought to do you for next Halloween.

MRS.
BALESTIER: You've been drinking.

BEATTY: Christmas.

MRS.
BALESTIER: Won't you ever learn? It's a disgrace – and it's against the law.

BEATTY: (*gesturing at Kipling*) Well, this gentleman's breaking it, and as he's the most respected man in Brattleboro I decided to follow his example. Merry Christmas, Rudyard. I see this cold snap has brought out the penguins. Doctor Conland, (*pumps Doctor C.'s hand*) I haven't seen you in a dog's age. Still pushing pills? Please drop in at Maplewood – one of my heifers is not looking at all well. (*to Kipling*) Since you're breaking the law you cannot decently refuse yours truly a drop of the stuff.

KIPLING: Quite right. (*Gets the decanter*)

MRS.
BALESTIER: Haven't you had enough, Beatty?

BEATTY: Hasn't he? Come on, Mother, leave me alone. (*To Kipling*) Something the matter with your wrist? Go on, fill it up.

KIPLING: Happy Christmas.

BEATTY: Here's mud in your eye. (*He drinks*) Hear about the avalanche on Monadnock?

57

Startled cries of "No!" "Was there anyone hurt?"
etc.

No one hurt. But the folks were frantic. I went
over there. I told them (*he smiles*) avalanche is
better than a whole lanche.

MRS.
BALESTIER: Beatty, where is Mai? And Marjorie?

BEATTY: They got held up. And a good thing too.
Rudyard's side-kick let it be known that my team
wasn't welcome in his stables.

KIPLING: The stable's full. Doctor Conland's horses –

BEATTY: He told me the same thing. I don't care. Gave me
an excuse not to talk to him. I like to walk – get
outside, blow the stink off. Don't you? But it's a
funny thing. I remember when I was building
that old stable. My nags got a warm welcome
then.

KIPLING: I'll speak to Matthew about this. He's not in the
habit of being rude to people unless provoked.

BEATTY: I find him pretty provoking. What do you think,
Doctor?

CONLAND: My relations with Matthew have always been
cordial.

BEATTY: Trouble with English servants is they give all the
orders. Matthew figures he's a cut above me, so
he sasses me. "Don't you sass me," I say – "I
ain't paying your salary."

CARRIE: I'd better see to the dinner. We're a bit short-
staffed today.

BEATTY: Don't go, sister. I just got here.

MRS.
BALESTIER: Yes, Carrie – stay for a moment. I'm sure it can
wait.

58

BEATTY: Have a seat. Your ankles will get all swole up if you just stand around idle.

MRS.
BALESTIER: Carrie's been anything but idle. She was up at six o'clock, preparing the turkey.

BEATTY: I was *feeding* my turkey at six. (*To Kipling*) And I imagine you were doing your chores, too, Rudyard. Slopping the hogs, shovelling out the chicken-run, tinkering with your manure-spreader. How is the old manure-spreader?

KIPLING: Empty. I was rather counting on you to fill it.

MRS.
BALESTIER: Beatty, for goodness' sake please light some-where. (*To the others*) He's always been like that – up and down, up and down. You'd think with so much nervous energy –

BEATTY: Yes? Go on, Mother.

MRS.
BALESTIER: I forgot what I was going to say.

BEATTY: You were going to say – "You'd think with so much nervous energy, he'd do something con-structive." Well, I built this house and you're standing in it, Mother. It's always the same damn question: If you're so smart, Beatty, why ain't you rich? It so happens I've got a wife and family, and if that ain't constructive, I don't know what is.

CONLAND: (*attempting to calm Beatty*) I don't think Rudyard would object if you had another drink.

BEATTY: I don't want any more of that British bug-juice. (*To Mrs. B.*) But if it was up to them, I wouldn't have a house. I wouldn't have a family. I wouldn't have nothing.

59

MRS.
BALESTIER: You're being impossible, Beatty. There's no one here who doesn't wish you the best luck in the world.

BEATTY: That's a horse-laugh.

KIPLING: (*to Carrie*) You talk to him.

CARRIE: I think you owe all of us an apology for coming in here on Christmas Day and behaving like such a skunk.

BEATTY: (*to Mrs. B.*) Know what they're proposing to do, Mother?

MRS.
BALESTIER: They're proposing to help you. I wish I had the patience, but I don't I'm afraid.

BEATTY: I know they didn't tell you. (*To Carrie*) You didn't, did you?

CARRIE: I told Mother all she needs to know.

BEATTY: (*to Kipling*) And of course, you didn't say a word. You were too busy tinkering with your manure-spreader.

KIPLING: I learned very early in life that to keep holidays festive it is usually necessary to avoid contentious issues, no matter what the provocation. I see you have a motion. I suggest, for the peace of mind of all concerned, that you table it.

BEATTY: You didn't say anything. You wouldn't dare.

KIPLING: James, please do forgive this unseemly eruption.

CONLAND: I was thinking I might go have a look at my horses.

BEATTY: Stick around, Doctor. I need an impartial witness. They didn't tell anyone what they're proposing – only me. And they thought I'd be fool enough to fall for it.

MRS.
BALESTIER: Why are you so con-trary?

BEATTY: Because they want to boot me out.

MRS.
BALESTIER: Then I have a great deal of sympathy with them. You've worn out your welcome at Naulakha.

BEATTY: Not Naulakha – Maplewood. Out of my own house! Out of Brattleboro! (*To Kipling*) You tell her.

KIPLING: This is simply untrue. He's misrepresenting what was a genuine offer to get him out of hot water.

BEATTY: Cowflap! I've got lots of friends in town.

CARRIE: (*to Mrs. B.*) We offered to buy his house at way over the market price, so he could make a fresh start.

MRS.
BALESTIER: That seems fair to me.

BEATTY: (*to Kipling*) Unlike you. You're the one in hot water here. Ain't he, Doctor? Know what they think of you here? Know what they call this house? The Crow's Nest!

CONLAND: Every town has its share of idle talkers. Brattleboro's no different from anywhere else.

BEATTY: (*to Kipling*) And guess who's the crow! (*To Carrie*) Tell her the rest of it. Sure, you're going to buy my house. But what do I have to do in return.

CARRIE: We told him he'd have to stop drinking and swearing.

MRS.
BALESTIER: He objected to that, did he?

BEATTY: Tell her the rest.

CARRIE: There was no rest.

BEATTY: That's a damn lie. After they bought the house I was supposed to clear out of town. Go down to Massachusetts with my tail between my legs.

CARRIE: (*to Mrs. B.*) He said he wanted to go into real estate. We offered to provide him with capital. Mother, he agreed.

MRS.
BALESTIER: Beatty, I cannot see why you're treating their good will with such contempt.

BEATTY: (*calmer, somewhat slyly*) They think I'm on my uppers, Mother. If someone's desperate, he'll accept anything. The fact is, they want to get rid of me, not help me. Doctor, who's been in this town longer, the Kiplings or me?

CONLAND: You, Beatty. There's no disputing that.

BEATTY: So I think I have the better claim to stay. Now it so happens that I've got me some money. Don't ask where I got it – I don't ask presumptuous questions like that. And, with this money, I'd like to make a counter-proposal.

KIPLING: (*calling Beatty's bluff*) We're always ready to listen to reason.

BEATTY: That's fine. Now, according to the newspapers, President Cleveland's getting het up about that Venezuela issue.

KIPLING: British Guiana. Go on.

BEATTY: And if it comes to war – which it probably will, and I don't blame Grover Cleveland one bit – your life won't be worth a plugged nickel.

KIPLING: What exactly is your point, Beatty?

BEATTY: In the event of a war – oh, it's coming – you'll be much safer in Canada. To speed you on your way and help your resources, I'm proposing to buy back Naulakha.

CARRIE: Buy *back*? When was it ever yours.

BEATTY: My land, my labor. But I'll give you a good price
             for it. You want me to get acquainted with the
             real estate business. This is the your chance to
             help me. My first transaction.

CARRIE: This is tomfoolery.

KIPLING: No, there's something in what he says. Let him
             finish.

BEATTY: Sister, you'd be wise to listen to this sensible
             man. I buy the house and the farm. You go to
             Canada – British Canada – and you're safe as
             porcupines.

KIPLING: (*bitterly*) He's tempting me, I must say. The
             Crow's Nest, eh? Well, this crow is more than
             ready to make wings to the rooky wood.

BEATTY: Only one thing. A condition. You play fair with
             me, I'll play fair with you. You've got to stop
             smoking that pipe. I'll provide you with a bucket
             of water. You'll have to stick it in. The smoke
             hurts people's eyes.

KIPLING: Now you're being preposterous.

BEATTY: (*unruffled*) Almost forgot. There's a lot of grizzly
             bears in Canada. You're a big tough man – you
             know all about grizzlies from England. I've got
             no doubt you can handle them. And Carrie's
             killed them with her bare hands. Both of you will
             be all right. But there's little Josephine to think
             of. You'll have to hand her over to me. Mai and I
             will take care of her, like she was our own.

MRS.
BALESTIER: That's enough! You've gone too far. This isn't
             joking any longer – it's abuse. I won't allow you
             to talk that way to the parents of an innocent
             child. Now apologize right now for speaking that
             way. It's a liberty.

There is a pause. Glances are exchanged. Finally Beatty speaks.

BEATTY: An uncommon silence. Okay, I'll tell you if they won't. They made the same goddamned proposal to me and my wife! Sounds crazy, but you don't hear them denying it.

CARRIE: I do deny it. We said no such thing. We offered to look after little Marjorie while he found his feet.

BEATTY: We'll keep her – that's what you said. It wasn't enough to buy my house and boot me out of town – no, you insisted on dismembering my family.

CARRIE: *(to Mrs. B.)* Caring for the child that's all.

KIPLING: *(to Conland)* I was going to give Maplewood back to him.

BEATTY: I suppose you can guess what my answer is.

KIPLING: I say, Beatty, this is the most roundabout way of saying no it's ever been my privilege to observe.

BEATTY: What you just said is pretty roundabout.

MRS.
BALESTIER: Where is Mai?

BEATTY: Maplewood. I made her stay put.

CARRIE: Beatty!

BEATTY: You two should thank me for that. She was raring to come over. Yep. With a tomahawk. "They want to kidnap my little girl!" And it's nothing but the truth. *(To Carrie)* Sister, you've seen Mai for the last time. And I rather guess you won't see me again – ever! If you're smart. Merry Christmas, Mother. Doctor Conland.

He goes to the edge of the darkness. Kipling follows him. Beatty makes a gesture of rejection, then speaks in a fierce whisper to Kipling.

64

BEATTY: Don't let me see the whites of your eyes, Redcoat.

Kipling flinches at this; but Beatty hasn't finished.

And don't let me ever catch you alone!

Beatty leaves. Kipling stares after him, then turns and speaks woodenly.

KIPLING: I think it's only fair to warn cook that we'll have two people short for dinner.

The rest hesitate.

Do go in!

All leave, except Carrie and Kipling. Kipling has turned back to stare in the direction Beatty has gone.

CARRIE: (*with concern*) Rud?

KIPLING: Corkscrews! Head-knuckles!

ACT TWO

ACT TWO

———

Scene 1

The distant sound of a train chugging away, and a train whistle, as Kipling and Conland walk onstage. They each carry a suitcase and a fishing rod, and are wearing light suits. It is a spring afternoon in 1896. They stop and look across the stage.

KIPLING: Naulakha! There's my ship – she does look like a ship on the hillside – beautiful –

CONLAND: Yes, she has a ship's lines – that long foredeck, and a bridge there –

As Kipling and Conland gaze and speak, Kipling wipes his brow with a handkerchief. Putting the handkerchief away, he slaps his breast pocket, then all his pockets.

KIPLING: James, I am an ass! I've left my stylo at Brooks' Hotel. (*Going over his movements*) "Much obliged if you'd sign our visitors' book, Mr. Kipling." "No, my pen's had more practise." Signed the book. "Here is John Hay's signature." Et cetera, et cetera. Then, the handshake – Masonic handshake – my mind fully engaged – and my stylo still on the counter. Undone by Freemasonry!

CONLAND: They'll send it on ahead.

KIPLING: And if they don't – if they forget it? I've got to have it.

69

CONLAND: Relax, Rudyard. You were just saying that Gloucester made a new man of you.

KIPLING: I'm superstitious about my working tools. I wrote my *Jungle Books* with that stylo. I'm going back for it. I'll use my wheel. I'll cycle down – yes, it's a lovely day – perfect for a turn on my wheel –

As he is speaking, Mary Hackett enters, as if in pursuit. Seeing her, Kipling turns away.

James, will you tell this tick –

MARY: I understand you've just come from Gloucester, Mr. Kipling.

KIPLING: (*to Mary*) I haven't the faintest idea what you're talking about.

CONLAND: You will excuse us. We've had a tiring trip.

MARY: From the coast? Gloucester?

KIPLING: Gloucester is in Gloucestershire.

MARY: I've just come from the station. I was going to meet your train. The one from Gloucester – you were on it.

KIPLING: You are mistaken. We were on the Boston train. The Great Western goes to Gloucester.

MARY: No, the Boston and Maine. That's the Gloucester train.

KIPLING: Not in England.

MARY: They said you were at Brooks' Hotel. But by the time I got there you'd left.

KIPLING: You appear to know everything. Tell me, where is my pen? Go on – where? Have you got it?

MARY: No, I – one of our reporters saw you in Gloucester.

KIPLING: Impossible.

70

MARY: Cape Ann to be exact.

KIPLING: He needs new gig-lamps.

MARY: He saw you fishing. With those rods. Did you catch anything?

KIPLING: An Irishman. By the seat of his britches. He appeared to be emigrating. We threw him back.

MARY: Is it true you're writing a book about fishermen?

KIPLING: (*irritated*) I have lost my pen!

MARY: Would you describe it as a novel?

KIPLING: I am not writing anything!

CONLAND: (*to Mary*) Why don't you send Mr. Kipling a letter.

KIPLING: I shall give it all the friendly attention it deserves.

MARY: (*in her defense*) You were a journalist, sir.

KIPLING: I don't give interviews, I have no news for your paper.

MARY: I can wait.

KIPLING: You can't wait here. This is private property. (*To Conland*) Why are there no hedges in this country!

Kipling and Conland continue into the study.

MARY: "Kipling As A Sailor Man".

She scribbles in her notebook, then leaves. Kipling and Conland put down their impedimenta.

KIPLING: So a train ticket's news these days. In this country, one has either to run one's own business or be bossed by any Irish hyena who can hire a printing press and get trusted for a fount of type.

CONLAND: You've got to admire her courage –

71

KIPLING: I do not care for beats on ten dollars a week calling them brother journalists and investigating my under-clothing on the strength of it.

CONLAND: They won't get anywhere if you don't give them a chance.

KIPLING: No law says I have to be nice to them.

CONLAND: I don't mean that, exactly. Getting mad at them is almost worse than running away and hiding from them.

KIPLING: I don't run. I don't hide. I'll fight them, if I have to.

CONLAND: (*affectionately exasperated*) And that's just what they want. They'll dish it up on the front page.

KIPLING: They'll be the losers.

CONLAND: (*reciting*) "When ye fight with a Wolf of the Pack, ye must fight him alone and afar,
Lest others take part in the quarrel, and the Pack be diminished by war."

KIPLING: (*challengingly*) "Because of his age and his cunning, because of his gripe and his paw,
In all that the Law leaveth open, the word of the Head Wolf is law!"

Carrie enters as Kipling is speaking. After his sententious lines, he becomes boyish.
Carrie is no longer pregnant – the baby, Elsie, was born in late December.

Carrie, darling –

CARRIE: Rud –

They embrace.

72

KIPLING: How are the cubs?

CARRIE: Missing their daddy awfully – Hello, Doctor.

CONLAND: Hello, Carrie. I've delivered him home in one piece, as I said I would. I could hardly tear him away from those fishermen. He wants to know everything about everything – he just sits and smokes and listens. Those old salts have never known such attentions. They think he's going to make celebrities of them.

KIPLING: James was right. I do believe there's a book in this. An American book for a change. What good people those fishermen are! We might have to go back one more time. I understand the cleaning and salting, but it's jolly difficult to get the rigging right. And they will insist on contradicting each other.

CONLAND: Not to say lying through their teeth.

KIPLING: By the side of these fisherman, Ananias was a babe in arms.

CONLAND: Rudyard makes the mistake of asking the same question twice. Which is why he always seems to end up with two different answers.

KIPLING: Not quite. But those captains are a rum lot. We met a certain Captain Frost in Gloucester. I asked him to tell me the most thrilling experience of his life. He told me how, in a storm, all his rigging had been destroyed – absolutely shredded. But he wasn't defeated – no, sir! He nailed his shirt to the mast and used that to sail proudly into port.

CARRIE: (*laughing*) I don't believe a word of that.

KIPLING: Wait for it. We then sailed to East Gloucester – Cape Ann way. And there I met a Captain Hawkins. "Captain," I said, "what is the most startling adventure you ever had at sea?" "Wal," replies the old mariner, shifting his quid, "perhaps ye've heard tell how a sea captain of this

73

port came sailing in after a storm with his shirt nailed to the mast?" "Yes," I said, "I've heard that." "Wal, sir," he says, without blinking, "that was me." I was quite astonished. I said, "I thought that was Captain Frost." "Mebbe, sir," was his unabashed reply. "Mebbe he did it too, but I did it fust."

CARRIE: Oh, Rud, it's so good to have you home. (*Embraces Kipling*)

CONLAND: (*embarrassed*) I'd better see to Elsie.

CARRIE: She's sleeping.

CONLAND: I won't wake her. I'll just have a quick look and listen and find my own way out. I've got some patients to see on the way home.

KIPLING: You've been wonderful, James.

CONLAND: It was a pleasure. (*He leaves*)

KIPLING: (*gesturing to the papers on his desk*) And now I've got these notions to sort.

CARRIE: Have you had your tea?

KIPLING: We stopped at Brooks'. (*Kipling goes to his desk, begins sorting through his papers. He speaks over his shoulder.*) Goodhue and some others were there. Uncommonly jolly. The tea was tepid. No one seemed to notice, what with all the raucous chatter. One thing about fishermen – no politics, no gossip.

CARRIE: There's gossip here. I'd better tell you before you hear it in town. It's Beatty.

KIPLING: Yes?

CARRIE: He's declared himself bankrupt.

KIPLING: Huh! Humbled at last.

CARRIE: No. He's been shouting it all over town. Crowing. You'd think from the noise he makes that

74

he'd struck gold on his back pasture. Why he's positively gloating about it.

KIPLING: Bluster, that's all. Deep down, he's ashamed and afraid, like the bully he is.

CARRIE: He wants to humiliate us.

KIPLING: He's only humiliated himself.

CARRIE: You don't know Beatty. He's no fool. Filing for bankruptcy is his way of declaring that we rejected him. So we're the heartless ones – he's our victim. That's how he wants it to look. He's asking for sympathy – and he'll get it. And we'll be hated –

KIPLING: All of Brattleboro knows I've been carrying that boy by the slack of his breeches for four years. If it wasn't for us he would have been bankrupt in '92. He would have been on the bricks! (*With concern*) We did pay him that forty dollars, didn't we?

CARRIE: Every last cent.

KIPLING: Then we're square. He's brought it on his own head. He can hardly deny it. No one knows better than Beatty how we've been squeezed. That drunken sailor could teach a Bombay Parsee a thing or two.

As he speaks he rings the servants' bell. Matthew Howard appears.

My wheel, Matthew. I have to go back into town.

HOWARD: Yes, sir. Lovely day, sir. (*He leaves*)

CARRIE: What is it, Rud?

KIPLING: My stylo. Left it at Brooks'. Masonic handshake. Stylo wriggled free. What were we talking about?

CARRIE: Beatty – the forty dollars. He worked for it.

KIPLING: Because we pleaded with him. If he had taken us

75

up in our proposal to buy him out he'd still be in our hair. He chose to abuse us for that. So now it's finished, and we're well rid of him. *El-hamdu lillahi Rub el-alamin!*

CARRIE: We'll never be rid of him. He's right down there, Rud. He's not going to leave Maplewood.

KIPLING: (*emphatically*) He's toothless. Like his friend Grover Cleveland. You notice there's no jabber about the Monroe Doctrine now. They were bluffing! More bankruptcy! It's Cuba's turn next, but Spain will do bloodily what we would have done mercifully, and the Americans will curse the day they rioted against us. These are terrible times, but I'm not going to spend them apologizing to heathens for beating the savagery out of them.

CARRIE: He'll fight, and he won't be satisfied until one of us is dead.

KIPLING: Then Allah give us strength. Beatty is welcome to his bankruptcy – it suits him down to the ground.

CARRIE: Please don't say anything in town. Beatty's so unpredictable.

KIPLING: I could educate him. And I think he knows that. Yes, I think the dear boy is finally beginning to understand my attitude.

Carrie goes near to Kipling and embraces him tenderly.

CARRIE: I'm glad you've got a book to work on. You're always so cheerful when you're working.

KIPLING: It's just a notion – not a book yet. If it grows to a book, it will be a good American one. Children will adore it. Their parents will say I've got all my details wrong. (*He smiles*) The details are Conland's, the rest will be mine.

He rises and goes to the window.

Thank God, spring is here. We can get Mr. Reed to build us that new barn. We won't have to plead with *him* to finish it.

Matthew appears with the bicycle.

Ah, that's what I need – a run on my wheel. I'll get my stylo and be right back. Thank you, Matthew.

CARRIE: Be careful, Rud.

KIPLING: It's all downhill.

CARRIE: It'll be dark in an hour.

KIPLING: I'll be back before then. I'll see the cubs to bed.

He mounts the bike a bit unsteadily and looks off-stage.

Glorious country around here.

CARRIE: You won't take us away?

KIPLING: America's not my home.

CARRIE: Rud!

KIPLING: But Naulakha is. We'll fill this house with children and buy them wheels. We'll be happy. (*Looks again off-stage*) Conland was saying there were once wolves here. But they went away. I suppose they lost their lairs somehow, with the coming of – what? (*He smiles*) American civilization? The white man? Wolves know best.

He begins to pedal.

I feel a bit drunken on this.

CARRIE: Balance, Rud!

KIPLING: (*sings*) "What shall we do with the drunken sailor,
What shall we do with the drunken sailor,

77

What shall we do with the drunken
  sailor,
Early in the morning – "

He cycles off.

*There is darkness, but Kipling is still singing and
jangling the bicycle bell. We hear, ". . . Shove
him in the scuppers with a hosepipe on him" etc.*

The rattling of the bike. The bell. Singing.

*Then, suddenly, an exclamation, a real cry of
fright, and a crash.*

*The lights come up at the front of the stage to
reveal Kipling sprawled on the ground with the
bike. He lies there for a moment.*

(*half-singing*) "What shall we do with
a . . . What shall we so . . ." My wrist. Still seems
to work. Blast. Oh, my back. Damn this wheel –
damn this road –

*As he speaks, there are hoofbeats and wagon-
wheels, the sound of a carriage approaching.
Kipling is still lighted, but there is darkness all
around him.*

Here's my ride home. How humiliating.
Trounced by a wheel – my wrist –

The hoofbeats and carriage noise.

Oh, lord – Beatty. (*Whispers*) Go away. He's
going – no, turning –

The carriage stops, the horses stamp and snort.

No –

*A thump, and the feeble light reveals Beatty
standing on Kipling's desk as on the bank of a
road. He towers threateningly over Kipling and is
very angry.*

78

BEATTY: See here – I want to talk to you! What are these lies you've been spreading about me!

KIPLING: (*frightened and in a little boy's voice*) No, please don't – I've hurt my wrist – look – blood – please –

BEATTY: I'm going to kill you – now!

KIPLING: Please! Put down that gun!

BEATTY: I'm going to blow your goddamned soul out of your body! You're a liar.

KIPLING: My wrist! It's broken! Look – please – no!

Beatty howls as the lights go out.

BEATTY: Liar!

Scene 2

Naulakha, the study, as before. Kipling and Matthew Howard enter. Kipling's wrist is cut – a bloody cloth is wound around it. Kipling, who is supported by Howard, is pale and shaken, but putting on a brave face.

HOWARD: Steady on, sir, you're doing fine.

KIPLING: I'm all right, Matthew. It's just my wrist. I've got my sea-legs.

HOWARD: I saw you pushing that wheel up the road and I knew something was wrong. It's not like you to be pushing! Take a seat, sir. I'll call Mrs. Kipling – she'll want to have a dekko at that wound.

KIPLING: (*taking out a clean handkerchief; Matthew helps him tie a new bandage*) No. It'll just upset her. I think I need some more lessons.

HOWARD: Must have been quite a tumble, sir.

KIPLING: More a fall than a tumble. How's the wheel?

HOWARD: Not bad. I can straighten the frame. Did you have to push her far?

KIPLING: Waite's Corner. No bones broken. Allah is merciful.

HOWARD: I don't trust those machines. Penny-farthings, bone-shakers.

KIPLING: I think of mine as the Devil's Toastrack.

HOWARD: Won't catch me on one of them, squire.

KIPLING: They're fairly reliable, in actual fact. And I know mine is still in working order.

HOWARD: Still in pushing order.

KIPLING: No. After I fell I remounted and proceeded into town.

HOWARD: You never did!

KIPLING: (*almost evasively*) I had some business to attend to. (*Regaining himself*) Coming back was the breezy part, don't you know. All uphill. And I opened my wrist again from the effort, round about Beechwood. That's why I was pushing.

HOWARD: (*going to the door*) What you need's a cup of char, sir. I'll see to it.

KIPLING: Don't go, Matthew.

HOWARD: Sir?

KIPLING: It wasn't the spill that shook me up. This wrist isn't serious. It was Beatty.

HOWARD: Mr. Beatty, sir?

KIPLING: He came to my rescue.

HOWARD: I don't understand, sir.

KIPLING: I was approaching the corner. My wheel hit a stone and I fell. It knocked the wind out of me. I lay there trying to regain my equilibrium, but before I could get up and dust myself off who should I hear tearing up the road but Beatty and his team of grays.

HOWARD: Fat lot he cares, I should imagine.

KIPLING: He went past me, then turned sharply and came back.

HOWARD: Wouldn't take him for a Samaritan, sir.

KIPLING: His role in this was unSamaritan in the extreme. He flailed his whip and I thought for a moment he was going to use it on me. Then he began cursing. I propped myself up on one elbow and said, as calmly as I could, "If you have anything to say, you can say it to my lawyer."

HOWARD: That's the spirit, sir! That's what the bloke deserves. All this talk about him being so friendly and funny is a lot of old rope, if you ask me. You took a tumble and he didn't lift a finger to help. Just like him, ain't it? You told him off proper, sir. He's no gentleman. I'll get you that tea.

KIPLING: Reach me that brandy from the shelf.

HOWARD: Right you are, sir. (*Pours Kipling a drink*) Wish I'd been with you, sir, I'd have given him what for. (*Hands Kipling the glass*)

KIPLING: Thank you. (*Sips*) That, unfortunately, was not the end of it.

HOWARD: I expect you gave him a piece of your mind, sir.

KIPLING: I've never seen him so angry. He was blue, Matthew. Sputtering, shouting. I daresay, he'd had a peg or two of this. (*Indicates brandy*)

HOWARD: But you told him, sir. "If you have anything to say, you can say it to my lawyer." Shut that Yankee gob of his! What he wants is a good hiding. Ought to be flogged. (*Howard paces with agitation*)

KIPLING: I was still lying there. His horses were stamping, their hooves near my face. He was still fuming, hissing like a cobra. He uttered some rubbish – (*Kipling throws the line away*) – some rubbish about my spreading stories, said he'd give me a week to retract. Stories!

HOWARD: That's menaces, sir. (*Pause*) He could be had up for that.

KIPLING: Yes. (*Drinks*) I asked him as calmly as I could if he meant personal violence. I told him he would have only himself to blame for the consequences.

HOWARD: By God, sir, he will. We'll 'ave no truck with 'im anymore. There's no way on earth I'll accept an apology from him. (*Pours Kipling another drink*) Why that must have been terrible for you, sir. And here I was thinking you'd only fallen off your wheel!

KIPLING: There was more.

HOWARD: More of that?

KIPLING: Rather. Delicate language.

HOWARD: He's an expert at that, he is.

KIPLING: His parting shot was something to the effect that I'm a no-good son-of-a-whore.

HOWARD: I'd do something, sir. Get the law on him. It's not right. That's threats, sir, of grievous bodily harm.

KIPLING: Yes, it is. But I made a good account of myself.

HOWARD: This is agitatin' me, sir. (*Goes to the door*) I can't stand it, sir. I won't have it.

KIPLING: Don't do anything, Matthew.

HOWARD: Someone ought to be told. Not me – someone.

KIPLING: Don't you tell anyone.

Carrie enters.

CARRIE: (*sees Kipling*) Rud, what's happened? You're hurt.

KIPLING: Not seriously. (*To Howard*) Thank you, Matthew. You might start straightening that frame, there's a good chap.

HOWARD: You call me, sir, if you need me. I'm ready. (*He leaves*)

83

CARRIE: Was it your wheel?

KIPLING: My wheel and your brother.

CARRIE: What's Beatty done now?

KIPLING: He threatened to kill me.

CARRIE: Rud!

KIPLING: He didn't make any bones about it. I'd fallen in the road – blasted ruts. He passed by. I didn't want his help, but I hardly expected a murder threat. "I'm going to blow your brains out," he said. He seemed to be carrying a gun of some kind.

CARRIE: How that boy talks! I'm going to have it out with him. I don't care what Mai says.

KIPLING: Keep well away from Maplewood, Carrie.

CARRIE: It's gone too far.

KIPLING: I forbid you to go to Maplewood. I don't wish to have this discussed. At all. By anyone.

CARRIE: He threatened to kill you! Oh, I know he doesn't mean it. He –

KIPLING: He meant every word of it. And that wasn't all. It was quite disgustful.

CARRIE: He's a boomer, Rud. Just a talker. I imagine he was drunk – drinking gives him such a foul tongue. But Beatty isn't a murderer. Why all he does is bark – that's his problem.

KIPLING: He's violent. Dangerous.

CARRIE: He acts that way – he thinks you're afraid of him.

KIPLING: I am not afraid of that dog. I told him so.

CARRIE: He's so pathetic. But that doesn't excuse his behavior. Accosting you on the road – and you were injured!

84

KIPLING: Bleeding. My wheel had folded. I could scarely see.

CARRIE: Something has to be done.

KIPLING: I don't want you to do anything. I don't want the servants to know. Matthew won't tell. It's too serious a matter to be gossiped about.

CARRIE: Then you admit it's serious?

KIPLING: Carrie, it was the shock of my life. I've never had my life threatened before. I was completely at sea.

CARRIE: (*holding Kipling*) Rud, love! Why won't you let me help you?

KIPLING: Carrie, dear, there is very little you can do.

CARRIE: I must talk to him. Of course he won't kill you –

KIPLING: I believe he would.

CARRIE: You don't know him. He's such a fool. But he has to be restrained in this wild talk.

KIPLING: He will be. Depend upon it.

CARRIE: (*sees the brandy glass*) Rud, you're drinking.

KIPLING: Sun's below the yard-arm.

CARRIE: (*distracted*) It's such a shambles. Mother would know how to deal with him.

KIPLING: (*almost playfully*) The boy is wild and speaking of murdering the stranger. What shall we do? Yes, tell Mother. She will deal with it. But where is Mother? She's far away – she won't be back for many a day. (*Pause*) I know that kind of suffering.

CARRIE: I'm at my wits' end. Neither Beatty nor Mai has even spoken to me since Christmas.

KIPLING: As I say, Beatty didn't exactly give me the silent treatment this afternoon. (*Angrily*) I will not have that jackal snarling at me!

CARRIE: He won't bother you, I promise. I won't let him. Rud, he's not capable of it –

There is a loud knocking at the door. Kipling, greatly alarmed, gets to his feet and takes the poker from the fireplace. Carrie is fearful.

KIPLING: Get behind me. (*Calls out*) Who is it?

CONLAND'S
VOICE: It's me – James.

KIPLING: (*quickly hiding the poker*) Barakat! Come in, James.

CONLAND: (*entering breathlessly*) Hello, Carrie. Rudyard, I came here as soon as I heard.

CARRIE: Isn't it hideous?

CONLAND: (*to Kipling*) It was ill-advised. You shouldn't have done it.

CARRIE: Rud didn't do a thing. He was lying in the road – injured. It was Beatty!

CONLAND: Yes, yes. But the warrant –

CARRIE: There's no warrant!

CONLAND: What in Sam Hill are they talking about then? The whole town's buzzing about Beatty's arrest.

CARRIE: Arrest?

KIPLING: Carrie, listen –

CONLAND: Rudyard?

KIPLING: There was an altercation. After he roasted me I proceeded into town on my wheel. I went to Sheriff Starkey's office and swore out a warrant for his arrest.

CARRIE: (*aghast*) Rud, you didn't.

KIPLING: That American threatened my life!

CARRIE: You could have waited – we might have talked about it –

KIPLING: I wanted to charge-sheet him while it was still fresh in my mind.

Kipling is brightly determined with self-justification. He turns to Conland.

You're looking uncommonly cloudy.

CONLAND: It's a mistake, Rudyard.

KIPLING: (*smiling, consciously quoting Grover Cleveland's threat in an American accent*) It's the law in these parts. I will resist his willful aggression by every means in my power!

CONLAND: The newspapers will have a field-day.

KIPLING: Damn the newspapers!

He goes to his desk and sits. He takes up his pen. Carrie and Conland look on.

Darkness.

Scene 3

The lights come up. Kipling is still sitting at his desk, as at the end of the last scene. He is alone, morose, his bandaged hand on his forehead.

Projected onto the back wall (but these could also be banners) are large, old-fashioned newspaper headlines, and some newspaper titles: the Boston Post, *the* Boston Record, *the* New York Herald, *the* New York Times, *the* Vermont Phoenix, *the* Boston Evening Transcript. *Some display crude line-drawings, portraits of Kipling, looking ferocious in his mustache. The headlines are lurid:* KIPLING ROW WITH FAMILY, KIPLING'S FAMILY TALES, RUDYARD KIPLING HAS BROTHER-IN-LAW ARRESTED, GOODBYE, GREEN MOUNTAINS, BRITISH AUTHOR IN FAMILY ROW, LOOKS AS IF LIVELY FAMILY SKELETONS WILL BE SHOWN, KIPLING IN COURT, A VERMONT DANNY DEEVER, KIPLING SHOCK ARREST, *etc.*

Beatty and Mary enter. Beatty, whooping and hollering, carries a copy of the Boston Post. *There are fragments of other newspapers stuffed into his pockets. Kipling does not look up.*

BEATTY: This is the best goddam thing that's happened in this town for a hundred years! You're wonderful, Mary. (*Kisses her*) But I rather think I had something to do with it.

Beatty struts around Kipling, yelling out the headlines we see.

88

"Kipling Row with Family"! "Kipling's Family Tales"! "Looks as if Lively Family Skeletons Will Be Shown"! I guess they will! And this (*slapping his paper*) – this is better than Petroleum V. Nasby. (*Reads*) "A Vermont Danny Deever – From an Unpublished Manuscript by the author of Tales of a Bungle" – a Bungle!

Beatty and Mary stand at either side of Kipling. In the following recitation, they ham, taunting Kipling and suiting the action to the word, Mary clowning with Beatty, marching him around, etc.

"What are the fish-horns blowin' for?" said the Copper-Ready-Made.

MARY: "To turn you out, to turn you out," the First Selectman said.

BEATTY: "What makes you grin so wide, so wide?" said the Copper-Ready-Made.

MARY: "I grin at what I've got to watch," the First Selectman said.

BEATTY AND
MARY: (*in chorus, with actions*)

"For they're arrestin Balestier, you can hear the town-crier say,
The lawyers form in hollow square, they're soaking him today;
They've taken of his neck-tie off, an' cut his spats away.
And they're finin' Balestier in the morning."

BEATTY: "What makes the Kipling breathe so hard?" said the Copper-Ready-Made.

MARY: "He's mighty scart, he's mighty scart," the First Selectman said.

BEATTY: "What makes his wife look down so glum?" said the Copper-Ready-Made.

MARY: "It's family pride, it's family pride," the First Selectman said.

BEATTY AND
MARY: (*as before*)
           "They're 'resting Balestier, they are marching of
               him round;
           They have halted Balestier, and his mutterings
               resound,
           An' he'll curse in half a minute 'bout a sewer dug
               on his ground.
           Oh, they're fining Balestier in the morning."

BEATTY: "His pew was right-hand pew to mine," said
           the Copper-Ready-Made.

MARY: "He'll see the village church no more," the
           First Selectman said.

BEATTY: "I've drunk his beer a score o' times," said the
           Copper-Ready-Made,

MARY: "He's drinking bitter beer alone," the First
           Selectman said.

BEATTY AND
MARY: "They are finin' Balestier, you must mark him in
               this place,
           For he said he would lick Kipling, you must
               watch him make a face;
           'Opprobrious names,' the warrant reads, 'tis
               Brattleboro's disgrace,
           For they're bailing Balestier in the morning."

           *Kipling rises as if tormented, crosses the stage
           and returns. But he does not sit at his desk. Beatty
           and Mary follow.*

BEATTY: "Who's that a-loping down the lane?" said the
           Copper-Ready-Made.

MARY: "It's Rudyard running for his life," the First
           Selectman said.

BEATTY: "Who's pawing up the dust behind?" said the
           Copper-Ready-Made.

MARY: "It's Beatty seeking brother-in-law," the First
           Selectman said.

Now they ignore Kipling, who stands aside and watches.

BEATTY AND
MARY: "For they've let loose Balestier, you can hear the quick-step play.
The bailsmen now have signed his bonds, and they proudly march away!
Ho, the village lads are giggling, they'll all hook jack today,
After bailing Balestier in the morning!"

During this last chorus, the headlines disappear, and members of the court have filed in. Judge Newton sits at Kipling's desk, the lawyers Hitt and Fitts at either side. Kipling stands uneasily beside Fitts. They remain rigid in semi-darkness, while Beatty and Mary are at the front of the stage, flood-lit.

Beatty and Mary laugh uproariously at the end of the chorus.

BEATTY: (*referring to his newspaper*) But what's this about me being "addicted to intemperance"? (*Pulls out whisky bottle*) That ain't intemperance – that's whisky! (*He swigs*)

MARY: You'd better watch out.

BEATTY: The arrest was a circus. Why didn't you put in the part about him wanting to go bail for me? The *Herald* did.

MARY: Because you told the *Herald* man. You didn't tell me.

BEATTY: He comes in cowering behind Haskins. Haskins calls me a drunken cuss. I say, "Hey, what's all this about opprobrious names, Sheriff?" "Fifty dollars bail," says Starkey. I told him I was flat broke, and then I look over and there's the Redcoat pulling fifty dollars out of his wooden leg. "Put your money away," I says. "I don't

91

want you to bail me out – I'd never hear the end of it!" The expression on his face was lobster sauce. I didn't need his fifty smackers. I've got lots of friends in town. I hunted one up and was free within the hour.

MARY: You said you wouldn't talk to the other papers.

BEATTY: Don't be a ninny. There are twenty-two reporters in town. They're paying me cash money.

MARY: I paid you cash money.

BEATTY: This case is going to make me solvent! I'm back in business, Mary, that was a hell of a poem.

MARY: I was mad. I went over to Naulakha last evening. That Scotchman was at the gate. The house lights were out – deliberately! They wouldn't even speak to me.

BEATTY: Can't imagine why. But you stick with me. What do you want to know?

MARY: (*takes out notebook*) Your Uncle Joseph Balestier came in yesterday from Rochester. What part will he be playing in the trial?

BEATTY: Good question. How much is it worth to you?

MARY: I've paid you!

BEATTY: Five dollars will get you what I told the *Herald*. Fifteen dollars will get you a promotion. Twenty-five and you'll be editor-in-chief. This is news, Mary!

MARY: All right, fifteen. When this case is over I'll need a promotion – out of this hick-town. (*She hands Beatty the money*)

BEATTY: That Redcoat is making me rich. Well, Uncle Joseph came in yesterday as you say. But I'll tell you something no one knows. He hates the Redcoat's guts. He'd like to see that little bastard hanging from that rafter.

92

MARY: (*taking short-hand notes*) What reason does your uncle have for hating Mr. Kipling?

BEATTY: You know better than to ask a silly question like that.

MARY: Maybe Mr. Kipling spread stories about him? Cheated him? Quarreled over a sewer? Called him a piece of Yankee pomp?

BEATTY: Take your pick.

MARY: (*writing*) "Yankee pomp" is probably the truth. Has your uncle given you any advice on how to fight the case?

BEATTY: Sure has. But it was mighty bad advice. He said, "Beatty, you can't go on with this. You mustn't. Think of your family." "Go on with it?" I said. "What the hell else can I do? Goddamn it, who's arrested anyway!" That made him see reason. But he's on my side and right now he's teaching George Hitt some special techniques for winning the case.

MARY: Beatty, this isn't worth fifteen cents.

BEATTY: Ask me anything! Go on!

MARY: Is it true that you threatened to kill Mr. Kipling?

BEATTY: That's false. It is a Christless lie. I met him on the highway and threatened to thrash him if he did not retract the goddamned lies he's been telling about me. They were based on financial transactions in which he claimed to have supplied yours truly with money. They reflected seriously on my goddamned character. How would you like it if someone was going around saying he was giving you money? How's that?

MARY: About seven dollars' worth. Some people say it's about a sewer. Is that true?

BEATTY: Cowflap. What are you writing? (*Peers over Mary's shoulder*)

93

MARY: (*reads*) "When questioned about the sewer, Mr. Balestier said it was arrant nonsense – "

BEATTY: I love you! But it is – arrant goddamned nonsense. It's his false stories and nothing else that have caused the trouble. You'll find that to be true when you hear all the facts. (*Peers again*) What's that say?

MARY: (*reads*) "With a look of careless unconcern, Mr. Balestier said – "

BEATTY: (*pulling out the whisky*) How's this for careless un-goddamn-concern? (*He takes a swig*)

MARY: So you think you have a good chance of winning this case?

BEATTY: (*slaps the newspaper*) Dearie, I've won this case already – thanks to you.

Looks behind him as the lights go up on the courtroom.

Excuse me, I must have a word with my lawyer.

HITT: Put that jug away, Beatty, and wipe that grin off your face.

BEATTY: George Hitt!

HITT: Have you lost your marbles? This ain't a burly-show.

BEATTY: Just oiling up.

HITT: They'll put you in the cooler for contempt if they see you with that.

BEATTY: The only person around here who's going into the cooler is him. (*Motions to Kipling*) For false accusations and spreading slimy limey cowflap about me. This'll be gone in two shakes. (*He drains the bottle of whisky*) Magic. I made it disappear. (*He belches*) Whoops – it ain't up my sleeve. Let me introduce you to Mary Hackett.

She's from the *Post*. She wrote that lovely poem in the paper this morning. Read it? "Tales of a Bungle?" "Who's that a-loping down the lane – " Ha!

HITT: (*to Mary*) Morning, miss.

MARY: (*to Hitt*) Are you optimistic about your client's chances of winning?

BEATTY: We already won. (*Gestures to the theater audience*) Look at all the people here – look at them smiling. This is a circus. You think all these people came here to see a local boy lose his shirt?

HITT: (*ignoring Mary*) We'll be starting soon.

BEATTY: I've got my speech all prepared. I copied it out.

HITT: Keep your shirt on. I'm not going to call you as a witness.

BEATTY: Why not?

HITT: Because I have a better witness.

BEATTY: (*he sees Kipling moving forward to talk to lawyer Fitts*) "Who's that a-loping down the lane!"

Fitts and Kipling move downstage as Mary, Beatty and Hitt move up.

FITTS: I don't know whether you're acquainted with the pre-trial hearing. Ever been to one?

KIPLING: Only in a civilized country. India. Some members of a Cult of Thuggee were being arraigned. It was not unlike this.

FITTS: It's very straightforward. Can't imagine why all these people are here.

KIPLING: I was saying to Carrie just the other day. There aren't any poisonous snakes in Vermont. But there are Vermonters. I prevailed on her to stay home.

95

FITTS: I don't know what to say about the newspapers.

KIPLING: I do!

Judge Newton raps his gavel.

NEWTON: We are not here to pass judgment, but only to establish whether there are sufficient grounds for a trial at some future date. The State's Attorney will read the charges.

FITTS: (*reading from a paper*) That the accused, Beatty S. Balestier, of Maplewood, Dummerston, Vermont, did on the afternoon of May 6th, 1896, wilfully assault Joseph Rudyard Kipling, of Naulahka, Dummerston, with indecent and opprobrious names and epithets and threaten to kill Mr. Kipling with force of arms.

NEWTON: What does the defendant plead?

HITT: My client pleads not guilty, your honor.

NEWTON: Call the first witness.

FITTS: I wish to call Joseph Rudyard Kipling to the witness stand.

Kipling moves center-stage. Hitt and Mary are in chairs to the side. Fitts is on one side of Kipling, and Beatty is on the other side, hovering.

Mr. Kipling, how long have you been living in Brattleboro?

KIPLING: I came here four years ago and made a home.

FITTS: What made you choose this town?

BEATTY: Tell him, Joe!

KIPLING: I was married in 1892, to Caroline Balestier, who had happy memories of the town. I had no home. When I had a look at Brattleboro, I thought: This is the place. So I engaged some men and had a house built.

BEATTY: On my land – tell him I gave it to you!

FITTS: Are you planning to stay here?

KIPLING: When I came here I had every intention of staying.

FITTS: I don't think it is necessary to go into your achievement as a distinguished writer of stories and poems. Not too long ago, there was an item in a newspaper saying that you were Teddy Roosevelt's favorite writer. That's good enough for us. So I would like to push on to Beatty Balestier. Mr. Kipling, how would you describe your relations with him?

BEATTY: It doesn't matter what he says – he's a liar. When he was seven years old he was made to wear a sign on his back. "Liar," it said. He told my sister the story. I said to her, "But it didn't cure him, did it?"

KIPLING: He used to work for us. When we decided to build, he had charge of hiring the men. He got fifty cents bonus for every man he hired. He worked pretty well for a while. The first six weeks he was with us he worked beautifully. After that he tailed away and didn't amount to much.

BEATTY: What did I tell you? Cowflap!

KIPLING: While we were on holiday in England, we put him in charge of the house. Naulakha, that is. On our return we found unpaid bills and every manner of disorder. I turned this job over to my coachman, Matthew Howard. This seemed to annoy Beatty, but it was all I could do.

BEATTY: Annoyed? By some silly geriatric English slave in a monkey-suit, helping this Redcoat pretend he's Sir Walter Scott – no, I wasn't annoyed!

FITTS: The arrangement caused friction, then?

BEATTY: You bet it did.

KIPLING: His conduct was not satisfactory to me.

FITTS: Did you continue to give Mr. Balestier sums of money?

BEATTY: Not a cent.

KIPLING: My wife has charge of our business affairs in the main. She gave checks to Beatty in payment for work.

BEATTY: Like I said – not a cent that I didn't work for. (*To Kipling*) Why don't you tell him? Tell him or go home!

Kipling turns to Beatty. He is confused by Beatty's presence and speaks haltingly to Beatty.

KIPLING: He was working off his debts. We went security on several notes of his, but he settled them up after a while.

BEATTY: Damn right. I was square with you.

KIPLING: That was in December, and that was when our good relations ceased to exist. The trouble culminated one night at our home – Christmas, in fact . . . I believe he was incensed about an offer of help I had made him . . .

BEATTY: Offer of help? You mean, kicking me out and taking my little girl.

KIPLING: (*to Fitts*) I had suggested that I would pay his creditors under certain conditions . . .

BEATTY: Describe them!

KIPLING: . . . I offered to help his family and care for them if he stopped drinking and got steady work.

BEATTY: What about buying Maplewood? Tell him.

KIPLING: I did not want his farm. I wouldn't take it as a gift. I offered to buy it and intended to give it back to him at a later date.

BEATTY: He never intended to give it back to me. That's an English trick. You think Britain intends to give India back to the Indians "at a later date"? The hell they do! And those niggers in Guiana will be waving the Union Jack until Kingdom Come. Thank God for Grover Cleveland!

KIPLING: But he rejected my offer. Thunderously. He said he didn't need me – he had plenty of ready money. (*To Beatty*) Three months later he petitioned for bankruptcy.

FITTS: Had you any inkling that he was on the verge of bankruptcy?

KIPLING: Apart from what we gave him, he had no source of income. He squandered his money on drink. Then he rejected our offer. Bankruptcy was inevitable. It is the consequence of foolish improvidence.

FITTS: Did Mr. Balestier owe you money at the time of his declaration of bankruptcy?

BEATTY: No!

Beatty stalks away and leaves Fitts to continue the cross-examination.

KIPLING: My wife would be better able to answer this question than I. She holds the purse strings. But I believe (*looks towards Beatty*) he owed us nothing. Accounts are settled between us. (*Confidentially*) But, dear me, we couldn't do anything about his drinking. He was seldom sober, and he was downright ugly when he was drunk. He always seemed on the point of breaking up. I was willing to talk to him, but he dropped me.

BEATTY: (*mutters from the darkness*) Cowflap.

FITTS: Let us turn to the events of Wednesday. Mr. Kipling, will you describe for the court what took place on the afternoon of the 6th of May.

The lights go down and Fitts steps back. Only Kipling is lighted.

KIPLING: I was out on my wheel – my bicycle. I set off from Naulaka at about four-thirty – I'd left my stylo at Brooks' Hotel and was intending to retrieve it. (*As if on a bicycle*) I was just rounding Waite's Corner when my wheel became trapped in a rut. I hit a stone and fell. (*He falls: the same posture as at the end of Act Two, Scene 1*) As I was lying there, I heard a carriage. (*We hear the horses, the carriage wheels*) I had injured my wrist – this wrist – I was bleeding. I looked up –

We see Beatty as in II. 1, standing with a whip on the judge's bench. Only Beatty and Kipling are clearly visible. Beatty is furious, Kipling helpless.

BEATTY: See here – I want to talk to you!

KIPLING: No, please – my wrist – If you have . . .

BEATTY: I want to talk to you now! What's that?

KIPLING: If you have anything to say, say it to my lawyer.

BEATTY: By Jesus, this is no case for lawyers!

KIPLING: Leave me alone – I'm hurt –

BEATTY: These stories you've told about me are god-damned lies. If you don't retract those god-damned lies, I will punch the goddamned soul out of you!

KIPLING: You'll only have yourself to blame for the consequences.

BEATTY: Do you mean to threaten me, you rotten little bastard!

KIPLING: Beatty –

BEATTY: I will give you a week in which to retract, and if you don't I will blow out your goddamned brains. (*Jumps from the desk and stands over Kipling*) Thief! Coward! Cheat! Liar!

100

Beatty steps into the darkness. The light remains on the sprawled body of Kipling, then darkness. A moment later, when the lights come on, Fitts is next to Kipling, who is standing.

FITTS: Do you believe that the defendant, Mr. Balestier, had any grounds for his accusation about the lies?

KIPLING: No, sir.

FITTS: No further questions, your honor.

Fitts steps back.

NEWTON: Mr. Hitt, do you wish to cross-examine the witness?

HITT: (*stepping forward*) I do, your honor.

Beatty joins Hitt, and Mary Hackett is close behind.

Mr. Kipling, the State's Attorney mentioned the fame you have earned for your way with words. But what he failed to say is that, as far as Brattleboro is concerned, the Balestiers are the salt of the earth. It is common knowledge that Madame Balestier, your wife's grandmother and namesake, has long been a pillar of the Unitarian Church right here on Main Street.

BEATTY: And she loathes this Englishman.

HITT: She is the grand-daughter of Oliver Wolcott –

BEATTY: – who appended his signature to the Declaration of Independence. Immediately after the signing, Oliver Wolcott went to New York City and distinguished himself by carrying a leaden equestrian statue of George the Third back to New England. He soon found a use for it. He melted this statue down into bullets, which he used to fight the British throughout the American revolution. He was a great American.

101

HITT:	And Joseph – Madame Balestier's late husband –
BEATTY:	He left millions of dollars.
HITT:	Nor was your wife's maternal grandfather any slouch.
BEATTY:	Judge Erasmus Peshine Smith had the signal honor to be appointed, by Secretary of State Hamilton Fish, legal adviser to the Mikado of Japan (*sings*) "Defer! Defer! To the Lord High Executioner – !"
HITT:	Judge Smith introduced the word "telegram" into the English language, and by shrewd but always fair dealings he amassed a well-earned fortune in his lifetime. This he left to his children and grandchildren. Were you aware, Mr. Kipling, of what an illustrious and wealthy American family you married into four years ago?
FITTS:	Objection. I do not see what bearing the Balestier fortune has on the event under discussion.
BEATTY:	It has everything to do with it!
NEWTON:	Objection denied.
MARY:	(*regarding Kipling*) He doesn't know what to say!
KIPLING:	(*struggling to begin*) I was well-aware that my wife's family was illustrious. I knew they played a part in the American Rebellion and had a record of public service and commercial success.
BEATTY:	Why call it the American Rebellion?
KIPLING:	That's what it was.
BEATTY:	It was a revolution. We drove you out, just the way the Venezuelans drove you off their border. Just the way the South Africans smashed your Jameson Raid. You're not having much luck these days, are you, Redcoat? What's become of all that talk of war?

102

KIPLING: We'll fight the Boers, if we have to. We would have fought you!

BEATTY: You had your chance. You ran to the Sheriff's Office instead, coward.

KIPLING: This hearing isn't over.

BEATTY: No. Carry on, George.

HITT: Were you aware that the Balestier wealth had passed to Caroline, your wife?

KIPLING: I believe it was equally divided among the children.

HITT: Millions were divided.

MARY: Everyone in town talks about how rich Carrie was before she got married.

BEATTY: She was rolling in it.

HITT: Mr. Kipling, you shared in your wife's wealth, is that not so?

KIPLING: (*to Beatty*) We pooled our resources, sir.

BEATTY: (*to Hitt*) Meaning he cashed in.

MARY: And he talks about the Irish!

HITT: (*to Kipling*) Pooled your resources, eh . . .?

FITTS: Objection, your honor. I don't see where this questioning is leading.

NEWTON: Denied! Proceed!

HITT: You told the State Attorney that you came to Brattleboro because Mrs. Kipling had had happy memories of the town.

BEATTY: Why didn't you go somewhere else? Why didn't you go home?

HITT: Or to the savage jungles you write about with such evident approval?

103

MARY: (*recites*) "For the wildest dreams of Kew, are the
                  facts of Khatmandu,
                  And the crimes of Clapham chaste in
                  Martaban."

KIPLING: I have found jungles in all sorts of places, even
           so-called civilized towns. I settled here because I
           liked the snow and the privacy. I have not been
           disappointed in the snow.

HITT: You expressed dismay at my client's petitition of
           bankruptcy –

MARY: (*reads from her notes*) "It is the consequence of
           foolish improvidence – "

BEATTY: I gave it all to him!

HITT: – Did I hear you correctly?

KIPLING: You did.

HITT: Is it not true, Mr. Kipling, that shortly after your
           marriage you became bankrupt yourself?

FITTS: Objection!

NEWTON: Denied!

MARY: Kipling bankrupt – I'm all ears.

KIPLING: The bankruptcy was through no fault of my own.
           We were on our honeymoon trip in Japan. I had
           wired all my money to a bank in Yokohama. One
           morning I withdrew ten pounds in sterling. The
           manager told me I could take more. I declined to,
           although I had a great deal in the account. That
           same afternoon I received news that this bank,
           the Oriental Banking Company, had suspended
           payment.

BEATTY: (*sings*) "To the Lord High Executioner – "

KIPLING: I was the only customer who felt the blow.

MARY: So he didn't have a bean!

KIPLING: (*to Hitt*) My credit was excellent.

HITT:	But credit is faith, not money, Mr. Kipling. Just as words are not deeds.
KIPLING:	It was the bank that failed – not me.
BEATTY:	(*to Mary*) Not a red cent!
HITT:	This occurred in 1892, and it was that year that you came to live in Brattleboro. A happy coincidence –
BEATTY:	It was no coincidence at all. Our rich family was here. I owned land where Naulakha is now standing. My grandma Balestier was at Beechwood – she put the two of them up. He just took what he needed.
MARY:	Loot!
BEATTY:	"If you've ever stole a pheasant-egg be'ind the keeper's back – "
MARY:	"If you've ever snigged the washing from the line – "
BEATTY:	"If you're ever crammed a gander in your bloomin' haversack – "
MARY:	"You will understand this little song of mine."
BEATTY:	"Why, they call a man a robber if 'e stuffs 'is marching clobber, With the – "
BEATTY and MARY:	(*chorus*) "Loo! Loo! Lulu! Lulu! Loo! Loo! Loot! Loot! Loot! Ow the loot! Bloomin' loot!"
HITT:	As a man who had just been rendered penniless you must have found this a very convenient refuge.
KIPLING:	My own set-back was temporary. But I do not deny that I was and am grateful for the hospitality and generosity of the Balestiers.
BEATTY:	I gave him land to build on – ten acres, with a mountain view.

105

KIPLING: Beatty was paid for his land.

BEATTY: A damn sight less than it would have fetched in a public sale.

KIPLING: (*to Hitt, as before*) Most of it was uncleared. And Beatty reserved the pasture rights to himself.

HITT: You bought the land for a song. Is that not so, Mr. Kipling?

KIPLING: I don't know about a song. It was a fair price.

MARY: (*writes*) "A nominal price – "

KIPLING: My wife made the deal. There were lawyers. There are records of this transaction. Perhaps the price was low. There were no other buyers in sight. All this is ancient history.

HITT: Four years ago? Not so *ancient*, Mr. Kipling. I thought words were your business. Well, you settled here on Beatty Balestier's land, and you set to work building a house. To whom did you turn to build this house?

KIPLING: Henry Rutgers Marshall was the architect.

BEATTY: He doesn't mean that!

HITT: And the laborers?

KIPLING: They were *habitants*. French-Canadians.

BEATTY: Tell him who hired them!

KIPLING: As I told the State's Attorney, I authorized Beatty to hire them and paid him fifty cents a man.

HITT: Beatty's land, Beatty's laborers, and I understand much of the work was supervised by Beatty?

KIPLING: Some of it.

BEATTY: All of it.

MARY: A darned useful brother-in-law, Mr. Kipling!

HITT: Had I such a brother-in-law, I would bless my

106

luck and be grateful for his help in my hour of need.

KIPLING: You might find it a mixed blessing, sir.

HITT: Let us dwell for a moment on the present. You said under oath that at the time of the incident on May 6th all accounts between you and my client were settled.

KIPLING: That is true, sir.

MARY: Give the date of the settlement. What was outstanding? To whom was it owed, and when was it paid?

KIPLING: (to Hitt) There was about forty dollars outstanding at Christmas. This was paid.

HITT: My client owed you forty dollars?

KIPLING: No. We owed him that amount.

BEATTY: Hear that?

HITT: You, Mr. Kipling, owed my client forty dollars? Now that is mighty interesting.

KIPLING: And he owed us work. There was a sewer pipe to be moved from his land to mine –

HITT: When was your debt to Mr. Balestier paid?

KIPLING: Round about January.

MARY: He's not very specific.

KIPLING: I was out of town a great deal – in Gloucester and Boston. My wife keeps track of the dates.

BEATTY: So do I. He's the only one who doesn't. (*Takes out a small notebook*) The forty dollars he owed me was paid on the 2nd of February.

KIPLING: (to Hitt) It might have been February.

HITT: Not January, then. And after that, you owed my client nothing, nor did he owe you anything. So I

107

think we can conclude that in February all business between you was at an end. There were no debts.

KIPLING: Or credits.

HITT: Just so. That is, let us say, after the end of February?

KIPLING: Yes, sir.

HITT: (*pouncing*) Mr. Kipling, is it not true that on the afternoon of March 22nd, and several times thereafter, you told Colonel Goodhue at Brooks' Hotel that you were carrying your brother-in-law, Beatty Balestier, by the seat of his breeches?

BEATTY: "If you've knocked a nigger edgeways when 'e's thrustin' for your life – "

MARY: "You must leave him very careful when 'e fell – "

BEATTY: "An' may thank your stars and gaiters if you didn't feel 'is knife."

MARY: "That you ain't told off to bury him as well."

KIPLING: I might have replied to the inquiries of Colonel Goodhue that I was helping him along.

HITT: And you used that precise phrase "carrying him by the seat of his breeches"?

KIPLING: "Slack of his breeches", yes.

BEATTY: And he told tales about me, what a drunken loafer I was, how I'd never amount to anything.

KIPLING: But I never circulated stories to his detriment.

MARY: He just said that he was carrying Beatty by the slack of his breeches.

BEATTY: I didn't owe him anything – he wasn't giving me anything.

HITT: And you used this same phrase – "the slack of his breeches" – when talking about Mr. Balestier to John Bliss?

108

FITTS: Objection. This is all hearsay, your honor.

NEWTON: Objection denied. Please address yourself to the question, Mr. Kipling.

KIPLING: I expect I told John Bliss, too.

MARY: And he told lots of other people in Brattleboro how he was carrying Beatty, how he'd done all he could for him, how Beatty was living on his bounty.

HITT: What earthly reason did you have, Mr. Kipling, for lying in this way?

KIPLING: (*confused*) You see, his creditors wanted to know what I was going to do about his unpaid bills, and that was unpleasant. I felt I had been supporting him for some three years. I was glad to see him working, but after a bit, he was not willing to work at all.

BEATTY: You hated me.

KIPLING: (*to Hitt*) But until his assault on me, I had only the kindliest feelings towards him.

HITT: You also told Colonel Goodhue that you had come to Brattleboro "to help the boy", meaning Beatty. You said that you had made this promise to Beatty's late brother, Wolcott.

KIPLING: Wolcott was a white man – and my dearest friend. I promised him that I would watch over and guide his younger brother. I came to Brattleboro simply for the reason of helping this poor boy, Beatty, and keeping him along the proper lines.

              Beatty laughs out loud, whoops, etc.

HITT: Then taking care of Mr. Balestier has been your chief occupation?

KIPLING: Incidentally, I have done some other things here.

HITT: What things?

109

KIPLING: I have written a thing or two.

MARY: And he's made a fortune out of it.

KIPLING: I have earned an average living.

HITT: Do you deny that you told Mr. Harold Jefferson only last Friday that –

BEATTY: "This Beatty business is preventing me from working. It is costing me a hundred dollars a day."

KIPLING: I may have said that.

HITT: Are you inferring that a hundred dollars a day is an average living?

KIPLING: No, sir, I am implying it.

MARY: I wonder what he paid those French-Canadians to build his house?

BEATTY: I'll tell you what he paid me! (*Takes out the small notebook*) April 12th, 1893 – $2.56. May 23rd, 1893 – $4.75. July 2nd, 1893 – $8.00. And so forth. And he was getting a hundred a day.

HITT: And you felt aggrieved to be paying my client small sums in return for work.

KIPLING: My wife paid him. They were ordinary business matters.

MARY: Ordinary business matters his wife takes care of.

BEATTY: Why did you quarrel with me?

KIPLING: (*to Hitt*) Then Beatty dropped me. You see, when I came back last April he wrote me one or two letters of an annoying nature.

HITT: But we have established that Mr. Balestier did not owe you money last April.

KIPLING: Yes, sir.

BEATTY: And I didn't owe him money when he told the town he was carrying me by the seat of my pants.

HITT: You had Mr. Balestier arrested without making any effort to correct the utterly false impression you had given of his dependence on you!

KIPLING: (*helplessly*) I've done my best for Beatty. I made an offer to take charge of his family if Beatty would stop drinking. This was rejected –

BEATTY: You were going to buy me out and rob me of my family. That's the kind of low English trick they use against blackies. That's the principle of empire – selling people down the river.

KIPLING: – It was rejected, although I had nothing to gain from it personally. It would have been a burden to me, but I was willing.

MARY: It wasn't a loan – it was a cash transaction.

HITT: It was a business deal, was it not?

KIPLING: On the surface of it, yes.

HITT: Let us go back to May 6th of this year. You described for the court what allegedly took place –

MARY: "See here, I want a word with you."

BEATTY: (*mockingly*) "If you have anything to say, say it to my lawyer."

HITT: Are we to understand that you had begun proceedings against Mr. Balestier before May 6th?

KIPLING: No, sir. It was a figure of speech.

HITT: That figure of speech, as you call it, is fighting talk, Mr. Kipling. But then words are your business. You had not spoken with Mr. Balestier for some months. All accounts were settled between you. There was no legal action pending, nor were there grounds for any.

KIPLING: He looked just crazy. It was my belief that he was crazy. He was blue with fury.

111

BEATTY:	Not red? Not white?
KIPLING:	Blue.
HITT:	If you think Mr. Balestier is crazy, why don't you have him examined and adjudged insane?
KIPLING:	I didn't know but what he would go raving mad right there and then. I should have begun proceedings to have him committed to an asylum for the insane, but I've been told that it is very difficult to have a person who is at times sane declared insane.
HITT:	Mr. Balestier's next words were –
MARY:	(*making the words sound reasonable*) "By Jesus, this is no matter for lawyers. These stories you have told about me are goddamned lies. If you don't retract these goddamned lies, I will punch the goddamned life out of you. I will give you one week to retract them or I'll blow your goddamned brains out."
HITT:	You told the State's Attorney that you did not believe that the defendant, Mr. Balestier, had any grounds for his accusation about the lies. In light of what you have said about carrying Beatty by the slack of the breeches, do you maintain that Mr. Balestier had no grounds for his accusation?
KIPLING:	Beatty's bullying goes back a long way. He lacks education.
HITT:	Beatty accused you of lying. Are you denying that you did lie to Colonel Goodhue, and several other . . . (*he uses the word with relish*) . . . sexagenarians?
KIPLING:	I admit that . . . I gave a wrong impression. Yes.
	During the following exchange, only Kipling and Beatty are clearly seen, Beatty moving cat-like around Kipling – Kipling crouching. Beatty looks more threatening than we have seen him. He has a whip.

HITT: Where exactly was Mr. Balestier when he accused you – and apparently with some justification – of lying?

KIPLING: On his carriage.

Beatty jumps to a chair. Kipling is beneath him.

HITT: At what distance from you?

KIPLING: (*apprehensive*) Hard to tell. His horses were stamping and moving.

HITT: He was seated on his carriage, then?

KIPLING: Yes, sir.

HITT: Was Mr. Balestier carrying a gun on Wednesday, when he met you?

KIPLING: No, sir.

Beatty flings down the whip and takes a rolled-up paper from his jacket.

HITT: Have you ever known Mr. Balestier to go about armed?

KIPLING: Not with a pistol.

Beatty taunts Kipling with the rolled-up paper.

HITT: And yet you were afraid of being shot?

KIPLING: I don't know as I am a man who is afraid of being shot, but I have a distinct aversion to it.

Beatty unrolls the paper. On it is lettered LIAR.

HITT: We are speaking of Wednesday.

KIPLING: Yes, I felt I was in danger of being shot.

BEATTY: If you don't retract your lies I'll blow your soul out of your body.

HITT: Although Mr. Balestier did not have a gun and indeed does not own one?

KIPLING: It was the first time I had had my life threatened –

113

Beatty still taunts him with the sign.

– I did not know the precise etiquette in such cases.

HITT: You made no acknowledgement that you might possibly be in the wrong?

KIPLING: He made no explanation of the stories which he alleged were being circulated.

Kipling is worried by the sign.

HITT: Please answer the question, Mr. Kipling. You made no acknowledgement that you might possibly be in the wrong?

KIPLING: I was not conscious that I had done Beatty any wrong –

HITT: You were afraid then, Mr. Kipling –

KIPLING: (*fearfully*) No –

Beatty shakes the sign at him: LIAR. He pursues him with it.

He was crazy – not in his right senses. He was shaking all over. I honestly think he would kill me if he lost his head some time. I won't be bullied, I won't be bullied!

Beatty tries to fasten the LIAR sign to Kipling's back. Kipling fights him off.

HITT: What was your response then, when Mr. Balestier uttered these cautions to you last Wednesday.

KIPLING: (*still grappling*) I was under threat.

BEATTY: Head-knuckles! Ag-ags! Brush-drill! Come here, Ruddy! Come here! Take your medicine.

Beatty manages to pin the sign to Kipling's back.

KIPLING: No – not that!

BEATTY: Take it back.

KIPLING: I won't!

BEATTY: You weed! Look at him blub – he's blubbing!

KIPLING: I'm not blubbing!

BEATTY: Head-knuckles! Corkscrews!

Beatty goes for him. Kipling recoils. They fight.

Go on – write to your mother – beg her to take you home.

KIPLING: No, no –

BEATTY: I'll give you a week to retract your lies, or I'll kill you –

Kipling tears the sign off his back and moves away. He screams in fear and anger.

KIPLING: I would not retract a word, under threat of death, from any living man!

BEATTY: (*as the lights come on in the courtroom*) He's running to Padre! Look! He wants to go home!

The courtroom has become orderly. The Judge at his bench, the lawyers at his side, Mary Hackett in a chair taking notes, Kipling where he was at the beginning of the scene, at the center of the stage.

NEWTON: Thank you, Mr. Kipling. You may step aside. If the State's Attorney is willing, we can have his summing-up. Please be brief. Mr. Fitts.

Kipling stands aside. Fitts rises and approaches the bench.

FITTS: Thank you, your honor. Mr. Kipling is a law-abiding man. It is clear from his testimony that a serious assault took place on May 6th. We have heard no testimony to the contrary. It appears that Mr. Balestier threatened his life and that Mr. Kipling had grounds for believing that this threat would be carried into action. There was,

115

moreover, no justification for a murder threat –
there can never be one under heaven. Your
honor, you cannot do other than to bind Mr.
Balestier over for trial for assault and for disturbing the peace.

NEWTON: Thank you, Mr. Fitts. I appreciate your succinct-
ness. Mr. Hitt?

HITT: (*with a large lawbook in his hand*) Your honor, I
have combed through the statute books – this
one, and many others. I have listened to what
Mr. Kipling has said with regard to his various
conversations with and about his brother-in-law.
For the life of me, I cannot see that any statute
under the law of Vermont has been violated. I
think my cross-examination of the witness shows
that the peace was not broken. The only person
present was Mr. Kipling, and he has testified that
he was not in the least worried about it. He said
that his only fear was in reference to threats. Well,
a threat, in order to be a crime in this state, is
made with the intention to do immediate harm.
There was no intent shown on Mr. Balestier's
part to carry the threat into effect. Words, your
honor, are not deeds. I cannot imagine which law
Mr. Kipling assumed had been broken when he
swore out a warrant for his brother-in-law's
arrest. Mr. Kipling, who is a stranger to our
shores, might have been thinking of some other
law – Chinese or Hindustani, or his own law.
Your honor, there was no assault. There are no
grounds for a trial.

NEWTON: Thank you. (*He leans back in his chair, looks
wise for a moment*) Having heard the arguments
for and against, it strikes me that this is a case
under the old familiar statute – of disturbing the
peace. I intend to hold Mr. Balestier in the sum of
four hundred dollars for his appearance before a
Grand Jury in September. Also, I think it would

116

be in order for me to demand a further four hundred dollars for Mr. Balestier to keep the peace. (*Raps his gavel*) This court is adjourned.

Judge Newton and the lawyers leave. Beatty and Mary Hackett pause down-stage.

BEATTY: What did I tell you? We won!

MARY: The only thing you won is a bill for eight hundred dollars and a chance to stand trial.

BEATTY: That's just a formality. That's Brattleboro's way of making you journalists feel welcome. Stick around!

MARY: I wonder if Mr. Kipling would give me a statement.

BEATTY: Ask him.

Mary looks at Kipling, who stands forlorn and a bit stunned. Seeing her, he turns away.

MARY: (*to Kipling*) All right, then, have it your way. Don't say anything. But you read your newspaper in the morning, just like everyone else. And you want to find something in it. I didn't invent him. (*Gesturing to Beatty*) And, sir, I didn't invent you. So, I'm sorry, but I'm going to the telegraph office now – there's no law against it. (*A bit sadly, and with sympathy*) If you don't understand why, no one does.

BEATTY: (*as Mary departs*) After you finish you know where to find me.

MARY: I'll see you in September!

Crossly, Beatty watches Kipling for a moment. Kipling turns to face him.

BEATTY: You lose, Redcoat. Surrender!

Kipling half-raises his arms in a gesture of friendship and forgiveness.

117

Cowflap!

Beatty marches away, smiling angrily.
Kipling drops his arms. He goes to his desk and sits. He is alone. Carrie hurries onstage.

CARRIE: Oh, Rud! (*She embraces Kipling*) Why wouldn't you let me come? Was it awful for you?

KIPLING: Disgustful.

CARRIE: There are some men outside who want to talk to you.

KIPLING: I don't talk to the press. (*Regaining his old dignity and annoyance*) Such an infernal bother.

CARRIE: Doctor Conland – Cabot, Holbrook, Goodhue, some others.

KIPLING: Americans –

CARRIE: They want to tell you they're on your side.

KIPLING: I appreciate the gesture.

CARRIE: (*hesitantly*) Will there be a trial?

KIPLING: It's set for September. A Grand Jury. But there won't be a trial.

CARRIE: September – a Grand Jury –

KIPLING: They'll need the witness – the white man. He won't be here.

CARRIE: (*understands what he means*) No!

KIPLING: This was odd refreshment. (*He glances around the room*) There are only two places in the world I want to live – Bombay and Brattleboro. (*With wolfish ferocity, almost a howl*) Savages!

CARRIE: (*attempting to calm him*) Rud –

KIPLING: (*quietly*) Let's go, my dear. (*He glances at the mantelpiece*) It will be night soon, don't you know.

Darkness.